The First 95 Years

The First 95 Years

The Memoir of Martha North

As told to Kate Leibfried

Printed in the United States of America
ISBN-13: 978-1718620292
ISBN-10: 1718620292

A project by Click Clack Writing, LLC
www.ClickClackWriting.com

Acknowledgements

Thank you to my granddaughter, Samantha Elizabeth Anderson Morales, for my ninety-fifth birthday gift: the opportunity to tell my life story to Kate Leibfried, founder of Click Clack Writing.

To Kate, for listening and writing this memoir.

To Janie and Kathy, for their edits and additions to the memoir, and their love and support always.

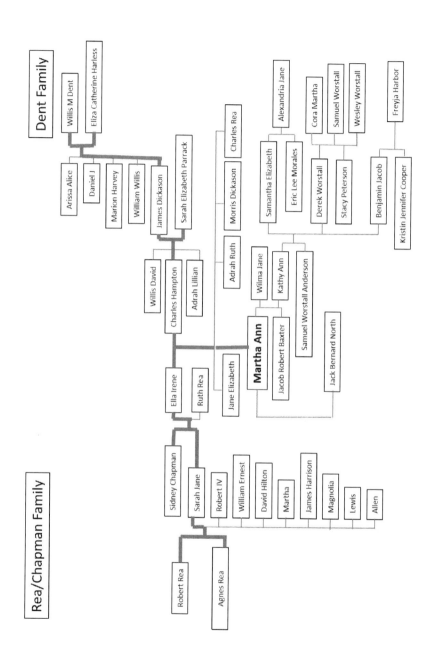

Dent Family

Rea/Chapman Family

3

Contents

Introduction

I'm a woman who has lived three distinct lives. My first life was spent in my childhood home of Montgomery, West Virginia and, later, with my husband, Jake Baxter, and our two daughters in Illinois.

After my husband's passing in 1969, I began my widowhood in Champaign, Illinois. I learned how to live again, independently, without a husband at my side. This second life was difficult and lonely at times, but I put my faith in a higher power and let God guide me to wherever He wanted me to go.

His path led me to my third life with Jack North. In the year 1985, at the tender age of sixty-three, I married Jack and embarked on yet another chapter in my life.

Through these distinctive time periods, I watched my family grow and shrink, I made new friends while treasuring the old, I moved across the country, and I traveled to many corners of the globe. My life has been anything but dull—at least to me! In every stage of my life, I've managed to fill my time with adventures, friendships, family, and stories.

I sincerely look forward to sharing some of those stories with you.

Part I
West Virginia

I lift mine eyes to the hills.
From whence comes my help?
My help comes from the Lord.
Psalms 121:1-2

I was born during the heart of the Great Depression in West Virginia coal-mining country. On October 4th, 1922, I entered a world I would rarely leave for the next twenty years. My hometown of Montgomery, West Virginia was only about two miles long from end to end, and stretched along the banks of the Great Kanawha River between two foothills of the Appalachian mountains. There were only six avenues in the entire town, and it was the kind of place where everyone knew everyone else.

This is the world that encapsulated and defined my childhood. It was a world of summer swimming, family sing-a-longs, and neighborhood games played in the middle of our street.

MY PARENTS

My daddy's name was Charles Hampton Dent. He was a hardworking man, with a tune always on his lips. I remember his sparkling sense of humor and the way he could make all of us laugh, even after a long day of work as an electrician on the railroad.

He was in World War I—known then as The Great War—and he rarely talked about his wartime experience. From what I understand, not many men did. It wasn't a pretty part of his past, and I'm sure it pained him to dredge up any war-related memories. From what I could gather, he worked on a submarine destroyer and sometimes manned the torpedoes at the back of the boat. Men had to launch them by hand at that point—something undoubtedly very dangerous.

The only thing he brought back with him from the War were his memories, letters from my mother, and a few souvenir pieces of rock from The Rock of Gibraltar. After WWI, it became illegal to remove any pieces from the Rock of Gibraltar because so many people were taking it.

Even though my parents grew up in the same area, they didn't know each other very well. My mother was friends with Daddy's sister, Lillian, and that's why they started to exchange letters while he was serving overseas during the War.

My mother, Ella Irene Chapman Dent, went by the name Irene. She was a strong and loving woman with long, silken hair that my daddy adored. She was a whiz when it came to clothing and textiles, and you could often find her sewing, embroidering, tatting, or knitting. She also loved to sing and, with my father's tenor voice and the harmony of her five children, she would often lead us in song on our front porch.

My mother earned her teaching certificate at the Montgomery Preparatory School and began teaching in town, while continuing to write letters to my daddy. When Daddy returned, the pair faced a dilemma. They had fallen head over heels for each other, but at the time, female school teachers were not allowed to marry.

They courted for a while and delayed making any major decisions about their future while Daddy went out to the east coast to earn a certificate from Westinghouse as a full-fledged electrician. When he returned, their feelings for each other were stronger than ever and, eventually, they made a tough choice: they decided to elope. It was the only way my mother could maintain her teaching career *and* her reputation. At that time, unmarried couples did not live with each other—it was a standard that simply wasn't questioned.

Fortunately, Mother and Daddy's families got along well. My mother, of course, was good friends with Daddy's sister, Lillian Adrah, and she also got on well with his older brother, Bill (known as "Pacer").

My daddy's parents were fond of Mother as well. Jim and Sarah Elizabeth Dent (whom everyone called Sally, or Sally Betsy) were dedicated workers and very committed to their family. I'm sure my daddy learned a good deal of his work ethic from his father, who was a store manager for the mines. I remember Grandpa Jim as being a tall man with a good sense of humor. He was disciplined and was the only one of his siblings who wouldn't touch alcohol. The opposite was true on my mother's side! Her father was the *only* one of his siblings who drank.

My mother was the daughter of Sidney Morris and Sarah Jane Rea Chapman. They ran the local grocery story, called Chapman's Groceries. In those days, the only place to procure foodstuffs was either at Chapman's or Kopper's. Kopper's was a cheaper option, and run by the mining company. The miners were partially paid in "script," which they could only spend at mine-operated stores, such as Kopper's. The script was not worth as much as government-issued dollars, since they only had value at a few places, and you really didn't want to receive your change in script.

During the Great Depression, Chapman's was the last grocery store in the area to run on a credit system. Many of the patrons appreciated the system, especially when times were tough, and paid off their debts without trouble. A few, however, took advantage of the system and would rack up huge debts at Chapman's, while strutting around in store-bought clothing (a rare treat for many people at the time!). After Grandma Chapman died, it was up to my mother to collect bills from those who had accumulated debt in the store. It was an unenviable job and many people simply never paid the money they owed Chapman's Grocery.

My mother was one of two children. Her sister, Ruth, was twelve years younger and absolutely adored my father, looking up to him as a role model.

When my parents eloped, they didn't have a large wedding with the customary dinner, gifts, and dancing. Instead, they kept the whole thing hush-hush and went about day-to-day life as if one of the biggest events of their young lives had not happened at all.

My mother, however, *had* to tell someone and decided to confide in her good friend, Sally Wisemiller (whom my siblings and I always knew as "Aunt Sally"). When my mother went to see her to tell her the news, Sally listened enthusiastically, smiled, and turned to a row of decorative plates displayed behind her. Taking one off the wall, she handed it to my mother and said, "Here's your first wedding present!"

That elegant plate was light blue with pastel-colored accents and was shaped to resemble a flower. I remember it being proudly displayed over the archway between our kitchen and dining room. Today, this treasured plate enjoys a new life. When my first grandson, Derek, was married, I gave the plate to his wife, Stacy, and him as a wedding present.

My mother must have had a way of attracting decorative plates to herself. One kind act she performed during the War happened to lead to a lifetime supply of them! At the time, she was teaching at Montgomery Elementary School, a young and enthusiastic teacher. She cared about her students just as much as she cared about her country and the brave soldiers who were fighting in the War. So, any time a troop train would stop in Montgomery (which was a frequent stopover point for the troop trains), my mother would march her students down to the platform to greet the troops and talk with them. It was a living history lesson.

One time, a young man waved my mother over to his window and held out a card.

"Would you do me a favor?" he asked. "I'd like to deliver a message to a girl who is back home in California. The message is simple; it says I'm on my way to Radford, Virginia."

At my mother's playful smile, the soldier added, "It's not what you think. She's my sister, and we have a code. If I tell her I'm heading to Radford, that really means I'm being shipped overseas."

My mother took the card with his sister's address and agreed to send the message. The sister was so grateful that she sent my mother a lovely hand-painted plate around Christmastime. She sent another with a different design the winter after that. And another after that. And on and on, for several years. I distinctly remember my mother's lovely, ever-growing plate collection—little treasures that dot the memory of my happy childhood.

When my mother went to Pasadena, California to visit my brother, Morris, she contacted the soldier's sister, and they had a wonderful time finally meeting face-to-face. My mother visited on one more occasion and tried to visit a third time, but the sister had unfortunately passed away by then.

My mother's inclination for collecting may be why I am the collector I am today. I have a large collection of Hummel figurines, Swarovski crystals, and cups and saucers. I also have a large spoon collection which started when Aunt Lillian received a third of Aunt Jenny Dent's collection of decorative silver spoons. Jenny's collection was started by her husband, Uncle Charlie. He would bring her a spoon each time he returned home from various cities where he stayed to "dry out" from his alcohol addiction.

Even though I've moved several times, these precious collections follow me wherever I go. How could I part with them? Each one is associated with a distinct, joyful memory.

GROWING UP IN MONTGOMERY

My childhood was defined by my close-knit family, a strong sense of adventure, and the rugged mountains that surrounded our valley. We lived in a modest clapboard house that kept growing and expanding throughout the years, like a living thing. We extended the living room, added bedrooms, converted the large pantry into a bedroom, and built a long awning-covered porch in front of the house that we often used for our family singing sessions.

The house was surrounded by a small yard with damson and dogwood trees. I remember the beautiful blooms of the white dogwood tree on the right side of our house, and the pink dogwood on the left side. The yard was framed by a wrought iron fence in the front and a row of hedges, which my father kept carefully trimmed at waist height.

Situated in the middle of town on 4th Avenue, we were able to sit outside and watch the hubbub of small town life. Sometimes, I felt like we were in the risqué television show *Peyton Place* with all the soap opera-like activity. We witnessed scorned lovers; drunk husbands; and people holding hands, kissing, yelling at each other, or gossiping about the latest pregnancy. I remember our neighbor, Mr. Nunley, would regularly run out of his house, chasing after his wife in his usual red long john shirts and suspenders. Though it was a small town, there was apparently no shortage of scandals.

Our home was also a hub of activity (though less dramatic!). Neighbor kids would gather there to play all kinds of games. We'd romp around in the yard, play in the sandbox, or take our games into the streets, where there was only a slim chance of a passing car. We'd play hide-and-go-seek, Red Rover, house, or any game we could think of. Since we didn't have sidewalk chalk at the time, we would draw lines for hopscotch in the dirt in our front yard with sticks. Then, we would toss a rock onto the board to indicate the square where we were supposed to jump.

It was here, running around with my fellow neighborhood kids, that I felt the first inklings of young, innocent love. I remember little Bob Miller sitting close to me in our red wagon and making my heart flutter.

But I wasn't terribly interested in love—or boys—until I was in high school. I was too busy with childhood games and adventures to bother much with love. That was more for my sister, Jane, than it was for me.

Jane Elizabeth was the eldest of the five Dent children. My family used to tease that Jane used up all the talent and didn't leave more than a few scraps for the rest of us! She was always poised, even as a young lady, and was good at anything she decided to try, especially singing and playing the piano. Jane was popular with the boys, and I remember her coming home one night from a singing gig, arm-in-arm with her boyfriend.

At the time, I had been climbing one of the neighborhood trees, as I often did, and spied her walking down the street. When she approached, I started whooping and shouting, "Jane! Look over here! Jane!"

Jane gave a cry and scampered away. When she reached the house, she ran to my mother and complained, "Martha is *so* embarrassing."

Looking back, I understand why graceful Jane would be embarrassed by her tomboy sister, climbing around in her skirts and hollering like a monkey! At the time, I didn't think much of it. That was simply who I was.

All of the five Dent children loved each other and got along well, even with the occasional squabble. Jane was seventeen months older than I was, and I looked up to her, despite our differences. We were followed by my sister, Adrah, who came along four years later. Then came our brother, Morris Dickason, two and a half years after Adrah. Then Charles Rea, two and a half years after Morris.

Since my brothers were quite a bit younger than I was, I would often babysit them or keep an eye on them when they had friends over to play. Years later, I asked Morris about growing up in our home and he said, "Well, it was a challenge sometimes."

"How so?" I asked.

"That house was *governed* by females!"

He wasn't wrong. After Grandma and Aunt Lillian came to live with us, the women outnumbered the men two to one. But, we all usually got along, and my memories of my four siblings are filled with laughter, singing, and escapades. One of us (usually with the exception of Jane) was always causing some kind of mischief, so it was a good thing my parents had an excellent sense of humor! I remember my daddy's humor very well, as he was always making jokes and cracking one-liners.

One time, my mother made his morning coffee. She preferred Cambric tea (essentially hot milk with water and a little sugar) and didn't like the taste of coffee. So, when she set the cup in front of my father, she wasn't quite sure how it tasted. Well, my daddy took one sip and started to prop up his cup with his fork and knife. My mother looked at him, perplexed, and said, "Charlie, what on earth are you doing?"

He looked at her with a grave face, expertly pushing back a smile. "This coffee is so weak, I thought it might need some help standing up."

That was my daddy.

I never did emulate his coffee-drinking habits, and I suspect that's partly because of an accident I had when I was a young girl. I was curious about the earthy-smelling dark liquid I had seen my father drinking, and decided I wanted to taste it. I remember reaching up and grabbing a hold of the handle of his coffee cup, intent on giving it a try. Wouldn't you know, I poured the scalding liquid down the length of my arm and began hollering in pain.

My mother ran to my side, assessed the situation, then sent Jane across the street to fetch Mrs. Kincaid. When Jane returned with our neighbor at her side, my eyes grew wide and I couldn't look away from the woman. You see, my siblings and I were suspicious that she was a witch. We kept our distance from her, afraid that she might work her magic on us.

Mrs. Kincaid approached my side and asked me to hold out my arm. I complied, quivering slightly, unsure of what she was about to do. The supposed witch grabbed my arm, held it straight, and began to blow on the scalded skin. Up and down, up and down, she coated my arm with her breath.

Then, she left. And you know what? That arm miraculously healed without a single blister! After that, the Dent children were more convinced than ever that Mrs. Kincaide was a witch.

LIFE DURING THE GREAT DEPRESSION

Even though we were born in the middle of the Great Depression, we never felt poor. My parents were hard workers, very resourceful, and never discussed money trouble in front of us. There was always food on the table and clothes on our backs.

My mother was an expert at recycling clothing. She would get old clothes from her sister-in-law, Lillian, or Aunt Ruth, and give them a second life by taking them apart at the seams, laying a new pattern over the material, and sewing them into something new. She might take a woman's dress and sew it into a dress for one of us girls. Or, she might take an old suit and redo the cut of it so that it would fit my daddy.

In those days, my sisters and I (like most women at the time) usually ran around in dresses, even when we were hiking up the nearby mountains. However, when the temperature dropped and the air grew too chilly for bare legs, we would put on union suits beneath our clothing. A union suit looks like something straight out of a cartoon—it's a one piece garment with a single flap situated at your behind, which can be closed shut with buttons. When I was little, I couldn't fasten the buttons by myself, so my mother pinned the flaps to the thick, cotton pants I wore under the lower half of the union suit. When the pants went down, the little flap would go down too! It was just one more practical application of her creative skills.

Not all of my mother's sewing was so mundane. Sometimes, she would design and sew costumes for our school plays. During one of the plays, another parent leaned over and said to her, "Your children and mine are the only ones with straight hems!" Other people must have also recognized her skill with a needle and thread, because it wasn't long before my mother was offered a job at the Montgomery Piece Goods Shop.

At that time, my siblings and I were old enough to be in school, so Mother decided that working in the Piece Goods Shop and earning a little extra income would be good for the family. She began work as a seamstress and bookkeeper. I remember all the colors and textures in that space, overflowing with bolts of material, thread, tapes, patterns, buttons…anything and everything you might need for a sewing project. It was a magical little world, and my mother thrived in it.

Miss Annie, the Piece Goods Shop owner, eventually wanted to sell the store. She worked out a deal with my mother in which the shop would be placed under my mother's name and Miss Annie would work as a paid employee until she had worked enough time to receive Social Security benefits. I don't know the particulars of their deal, but that's how my mother became a small business owner!

Needless to say, store-bought clothing was not present in our household for a long time. Because of my mother's sewing genius and our tight budget, the Dent children only wore handmade garments. That wasn't too unusual at the time, but still, I sometimes caught myself wishing I could buy a commercially-made dress someday, like the ones I'd see in catalogs or on the backs of the handful of wealthy people in the area. My wish for a store-bought dress wasn't granted until I received a high school graduation gift of a white nylon dress with a multi-colored belt. And *that* was for a very special occasion, indeed.

Though my mother wasn't quite as enthusiastic about cooking as she was about sewing, she knew her way around the kitchen and was inventive with the food we had access to. She'd often make meatloaf or

Swiss steak—two dishes she taught me to make, and which I've often cooked in my adult life.

One of our household's favorite meals was a dish my mother invented, which she dubbed "American spaghetti." It's a kind of casserole that involves frying up bacon (nice and crispy), along with onions, green peppers, and celery. This mix of vegetables and bacon is then layered in a baking dish with cooked noodles, canned tomatoes, and Velveeta cheese. These layers are repeated a few times, then baked. The result is always mouth-watering. Today, we call my mother's American spaghetti "Mother's spaghetti," in her honor.

My daddy was just as resourceful as my mother, but in a different way. He would collect coal along the railroad tracks that we could later use in our coal-burning stove or store in our shed. He was also handy with construction, and when Grandma Dent came to live with us, he converted our large pantry into a bedroom for her. Eventually, Aunt Lillian also lived with us, and he reconfigured the house to make room for her as well.

Though he worked long hours on the railroad, Daddy never failed to make time for his family. I have fond memories of him singing and teaching us to swim. He was a family man at heart, and always showered us with love. On Christmas mornings, I recall my mother shaking us awake and urging us to get up to open presents from under the tree before Daddy had to rush off and catch the six o'clock train to work. My Aunt Lillian, Aunt Ruth, and Grandma would join us while we opened our gifts.

Each of us would receive one present each from my parents, in addition to a few small gifts from aunts and uncles. We also had stockings, which usually contained a small toy and an orange, which was a rare treat in those days. We didn't have access to a lot of fruit and quite often fruit was only available during a certain season—strawberries in the spring, for example, or apples and pumpkins in the fall.

After our early-morning Christmas celebrations, my daddy would dutifully hop on the train to work. Though he had to rise early and work hard, he never complained about the sacrifices he made. During those days of national Depression, it was a blessing just to have a job.

The Dent children rarely complained either. We felt fulfilled and happy, even though we didn't have access to several "modern" conveniences, store-bought clothing, or special foods. We didn't have a car, a *real* radio, or even a newspaper subscription. Our home had a single bathroom that all seven of us shared (something almost unimaginable today!).

Summers were hot, as air conditioning hadn't yet been invented, and winters were cold, with just a coal fireplace to heat the living room. We had small gas stoves in the second bedroom and a humidifying radiator in the back bedroom to help with Charles Rea's asthma. With limited resources at our disposal, it was up to us to find our own methods of cooling down or warming up. In the summer, we'd often jump into the nearby river and go swimming; in the winter we'd bundle up in our one-piece union suits under layers of clothing.

With the change of the seasons, different vendors would pass through town. This was the era of traveling salesmen. They would sell home goods, medical supplies, jewelry, toys…almost anything you can imagine out of the backs of their cars. I remember one man who was a professional photographer and passed through town one or two times each year. He specialized in portraits, and we could pay to have our photos taken, sometimes with the pony he brought with him and used as a prop!

We were the only family on our block to own a set of Compton's Encyclopedias. It was an ever-growing collection—each year Compton's would send out an annual update book to add to the set. Those encyclopedias were put to good use, because all the neighborhood kids would come by to use them and to receive homework help from my mother.

In those days, people also made a living by running errands for families around town. I remember the "grocery man" coming to our home almost every day to take our order for any food we might need. Not everyone had reliable refrigeration, so this was one way to make sure you were getting fresh supplies. Of course, we were quite limited on what we could purchase from the grocery store in those days. Certain fruits were only available during the summer or early autumn months, and some tropical fruits, like pineapple, were very rare to see. As for milk? Fresh milk was expensive in Depression-era West Virginia, so we'd usually buy it in cans (although I do remember the occasional bottle of milk delivered by horse and buggy to our doorstep). Most people used a colored card in their window to indicate how much ice our iceman, Bernie Jackson, was to deliver—one color for twenty-five pounds, one color for fifty pounds and another color for seventy-five pounds. The kids would sometimes follow his truck down the street to get the ice chips he would hand us out of his truck.

The Dent children rarely ate candy, and when we did we would savor it like the special treat it was. That's why I always chose Butterfingers whenever I was lucky enough to get a candy bar—I could suck the chocolate off the outside of the bar and still have the buttery candy middle remaining.

Although my parents didn't spend money on luxuries, some of our neighbors did. Most of the people of Montgomery were kind and willing to share their blessings. One generous family invited us to stop by once each week to listen to their radio. Only one of the five Dent children was allowed to accompany Grandma to their house, and we always felt lucky if we were the one who was selected. At home, all we had was a crystal set, which is a simple radio receiver that we had to listen to with earphones because the sound was so weak. Only one person could listen to the crystal set at a time, so it wasn't nearly as fun as the neighbor's *actual* radio.

I remember walking over to the neighbor's home and settling down in the living room. We would all arrange ourselves in front of the large, stand-up radio and wait for the next show to stream through the airwaves. Usually, we'd just listen to Amos and Andy (a legendary comedy program), but sometimes we'd stay for Fibber McGee and Molly. Can you imagine two families getting together and doing such a thing today?

But those were simpler times—times before people had televisions, times before boom boxes, portable music players, the internet, and smart phones.

We had two other generous neighbors who welcomed the Dent children into their homes and let us read their weekly "funny papers." These two couples—the Champs (who owned a lumber company) and the Edwards—did not have children and treated us as their own. Each couple subscribed to a different newspaper, so we *had* to read both sets of funny papers! Every Sunday, my siblings and I would go—two or three of us at a time—first to one neighbor's house, then the other. We would pore over the comics, laughing at the antics of Maggie and Jiggs, The Gumps, Joe Palooka, and the Katzenjammer Kids.

Other entertainment in those days was the traveling kind—performers that would temporarily stop in our town and provide us with a few days of amusements. About once every year, a traveling minstrel show would set up a stage in town. The performers would paint their faces, play music, and perform comedy sketches. Occasionally, they would also hold dance competitions, which I sometimes participated in, dancing the Charleston or other fashionable dances of the time.

In the summer, a showboat would arrive from down river and dock on the shore for a few days. The showboats could only go as far as Gauley Bridge, where the New River and the Gauley Rivers converged, and the water careened down in an area known as "Fall's View." Then, the boat would have to turn around and make the journey back north. The musicians and actors performed shows for the town and I could hear the music from our house, but I was never allowed to watch. Apparently, the material was a little risqué for those days.

Another thing I did *not* have a chance to see was a herd of elephants on the night they passed through our town. Montgomery was too small to host a traveling circus, but some of the larger towns nearby did have the circus stop and set up camp. Apparently, the circus was having difficulties with their elephants and, one night, the animals refused to get on the boat to go to the next town. The circus operators decided that the only thing to do was to let the elephants swim across the Kanawha River in the middle of the night and walk through our little town! I didn't have a chance to see the spectacle, but I heard all about it later. In our little town, the elephants were a hint of the big, exotic world that lay beyond the edges of the mountains.

TRAIN TRIPS

In those days, we didn't have the means to travel overseas (let alone to the other side of the country), but we were able to see a sliver of the world beyond Montgomery. Because my father worked as an electrician on the railroad, he was granted several train passes each year that he and the family could use. Back then, it was a special treat to travel outside of the valley. Since we didn't have a car, or a horse and buggy (although travel by horse was quickly becoming obsolete), we relied on the train for long-distance travel.

Every summer, I would accompany my Grandma Dent to Roanoke, Virginia to visit her brother and niece, Thermutis (my daddy's cousin, whom everyone called Moody), Moody's husband, Charlie, and their children: Esther, Owen, and David. I was enthusiastic about train travel and became good friends with Esther, so it was always me (of all the Dent siblings) that accompanied Grandma Dent on the journey to Roanoke. It was a tradition that started in fifth or sixth grade and lasted through college. This precious time—these annual six weeks in Virginia—was a chance to broaden my perspectives, learn about life outside West Virginia, and simply have fun.

Grandma Dent and I would take the B&O train from across the river to Clifton Forge, Virginia. Sometimes, cousin Esther would be with me on the train (we alternated staying with each other's family homes throughout the summer), and we would pass the time arranging our dolls and playing with them on the bench seat across from us, while Grandma Dent dozed or knitted in another nearby seat. I remember the conductor taking an interest in us and commenting on our creativity.

There was no such thing as iPads or portable music players, of course, so we had to use our imaginations to pass the time. Sometimes, we would simply sit and watch the passing scenery fly by—the thick deciduous forests, the mountains, and the occasional farm dotted with cows or horses.

After about six hours on the train, the Wade Family—Esther's family—would often meet us in Clifton Forge, Virginia, and we would travel on to Roanoke together. To me, this was a bustling place, full of adventure. The family lived right in town, close to the kids' school, and I was impressed by their home and the fact that they had a car.

For entertainment, Esther and I would sometimes take the bus to the movie house and watch movies on the big screen. Or, we would play with dolls, explore the valley, or visit other nearby family members.

One family member who lived close to Roanoke was my daddy's cousin, Annie. I remember rolling into Annie's farm for the first time and being greeted by her young son, Lee. Lee led us across the field and over to a woman who was working the field. When we were close enough to see what she was wearing, I'm certain my jaw dropped and my eyes bugged. This large woman—my dad's cousin—was clad in old overalls and a big straw hat! In my world, women mostly wore dresses and skirts, and certainly never wore overalls. When I discovered that cousin Annie also smoked a pipe, you could have knocked me over with a feather! How could I possibly be related to someone like that?

Annie's farm also exposed me to the wonder of white watermelon. Along with raising sheep and some other animals, Annie's family grew a few different crops, including a particular type of watermelon whose flesh was the color of fresh snow. The white watermelon was juicy and sweet...and I have never encountered one since!

When I wasn't traveling in or around Roanoke in the summer, I was home in Montgomery, passing the time with my siblings and cousin Esther. Esther's father, Charlie, also worked on the railroad, so their family received passes every year as well. I'm not quite certain what his occupation was, but I do know he was an inventor. He loved to tinker with mechanics and actually invented something that Norfolk Western Rail began to use (he unfortunately didn't earn a penny from his invention).

In Montgomery, I have fond memories of playing with Esther underneath the damson plum tree in our backyard. We would drag our dolls and all their accessories and homemade furniture into the yard and create a playhouse wonderland at the base of that tree. Our dolls were made entirely of glass and only their arms moved, as they were fastened together with an elastic band. Before these glass dolls (which ended up getting a bit battered with time), I also had larger dolls with porcelain heads and cloth bodies and, later, dolls with wooden heads and rubber bodies. They were much different than the dolls of today—much less interactive!

We'd manufacture rooms for our dolls and furniture out of the orange and white Coty Powder boxes given to us by Aunt Lillian. We'd furnish the rooms with spool boxes (which became beds) and empty wooden thread spools (which became tables) from Mary, who ran the millinery shop in town. We'd also pick up scraps of material from Mary and use them to sew clothes for the dolls. At that time, we had to get creative with our fun. There was no manufactured doll furniture or doll clothing at that time.

When we weren't playing with our dolls, we were having some kind of an adventure, like hiking (always clad in skirts and flimsy sandals) or swimming in the Kanawha River or the natural pools that could be found in the mountains.

Those were times of simple joys, and I was happy to spend them with Esther, who was more than just a second cousin to me. We were close as sisters, and I saw her every summer until 1943, when she went into the service as an army nurse.

Another place I occasionally visited by train was our state capital: Charleston, West Virginia. Sometimes my mother, sisters, and I would hop on the train and follow the river north to Charleston for a day of shopping and wandering around the city. It was a place that was full of life. The city teemed with people, department stores, soda fountains, restaurants, jewelry shops…anything you could imagine. Cars and trolleys bumped down the streets, alongside the occasional horse and buggy. Perched at the river's edge, the alabaster pillars of the state capitol reflected in the water and its golden dome gleamed. It was a city that took my breath away.

Since it was a short train trip to Charleston, many Montgomery residents would travel there to make special purchases, such as store-bought clothing or jewelry. We would usually make the trip once each year—just my mother and the girls—and we would spend the day shopping in The Diamonds department store for Christmas presents and simply enjoying the hubbub of the city.

We would eat lunch in Charleston and were exposed to all kinds of "exotic" things, like real milk served in a glass. I remember my sister, Adrah, being suspicious of the milk the waitress set in front of her and demanding that it come in a bottle! The only milk she knew (that didn't come from a can) was delivered in glass bottles.

We would also often visit with Aunt Kathleen and Uncle Bill during these trips. She worked in the capitol building, and he worked in a men's clothing store. Their son, James Dent, graduated from West Virginia University, became a journalist for the *Charleston Gazette*, and has authored several books.

These were special times—the small moments that the Dent women spent together. My sisters and I loved and admired Mother, despite our occasional squabbles, and always enjoyed the times we spent with her.

I remember her long hair that she kept twisted in a bun at the nape of her neck throughout the day, and let down in the evening. One of her great pleasures was having her hair brushed, and my sisters and I would take turns running a brush through it while she told us fairytales and other stories. She fell asleep once—right in the middle of telling the story of the Three Little Pigs! The rhythm of the hairbrush through her mane soothed her right to sleep.

Daddy loved my mother's hair too, and when she was thinking about cutting it, she worried about what he would think. She decided to call him *before* cutting her hair to test the waters. When Daddy picked up the phone, she said, "I want you to know...I cut my hair."

After a few seconds, my daddy responded, "Well, what are you telling me for?"

Essentially, she was free to do whatever she pleased. Daddy wasn't going to stop her. That's the kind of man he was—very supportive of the independence of his daughters and wife.

So, my mother cut her hair into an elegant bob that hung almost to her shoulders. Although it looked nice, my sisters and I lost one of the activities we used to do exclusively with my mother—we were never again able to brush that long hair.

ADVENTURES

Most of our entertainment was free in those days. Although we found amusement in the occasional radio program or funny paper, we mostly just enjoyed each other's company. Believe me, in a house filled with five spirited kids, that is usually enough!

My parents encouraged our adventurous spirits and allowed us to take hikes or go swimming. We appreciated the breathtaking beauty of the wilderness that surrounded our home—the tree-lined Appalachian foothills, the churning river. In the fall, the mountains would blaze crimson, orange, and sunshine yellow. I loved taking long hikes up the mountain slopes, despite running into the occasional snake!

We would sometimes climb up to Lover's Leap—a jutting cliff supposedly named for the young American Indian lovers from different tribes who took their own lives by jumping off, hand-in-hand. Looking out from the towering cliff, I didn't doubt the story was true.

Other times, we would walk to an old abandoned cabin that sat high up the mountain. I sometimes wondered about the cabin's story and who lived there before they left it to rot in the wilderness.

Many of my adventures were alongside my siblings, but I also spent a good deal of time with the friends I had made through church or school. My best friend in town was Eileen Petty, and we did just about everything together. She was also in band, in the "Girl Reserves," and on the yearbook committee with me. From hiking to swimming to sleepovers, we were a major part of each other's lives from grade school, on. My other best friend, Margie DeLong, did not live in town. She took the bus in to school, earning her the title as one of the "bus students." The nickname wasn't a kind one. The bus students came in from the nearby mining camps and were thought of as "lower class." I didn't like the harsh treatment toward the bus students and tried to be as nice to them as possible.

Being stubborn as I was, I usually stuck to my guns and tried to be a loyal friend, no matter what. One time in Junior High, I was invited to a party by a fellow student named Mary Bowles. I was eager to go…until I found out that she hadn't invited one of my good friends. Out of principle, I refused to go to the party, but my friend and I decided to go out that night, sneak up to the house, and peep in the window while the party was going on. They were playing some kind of kissing game with boys and girls. When I got home that night, my mother met me at the door.

"Now, what have you been up to?" she asked.

When I told her, she was horrified and made me go to the Bowles' home the next day and apologize to Mary's mother for being "a peeping Tom!"

It was hard for me, but my mother was a stickler for what was right and what was wrong, and I knew there was no way she would let me off the hook. Fortunately, Mrs. Bowles was gracious about the whole thing and forgave me for spying on the party.

* * *

Some of my favorite childhood adventures involved swimming in the nearby river. Daddy taught all the Dent children to swim and passed his love of the water down to us. He was an excellent swimmer and diver and, when I was little, I used to wrap myself around his back while he dove into the water. I was the only sibling who dared to try it!

Our favorite places to swim were called Deep Water and Blue Hole. I liked Deep Water best when I was growing up because Blue Hole was frequented by older kids who didn't like to splash around and be goofy in the water, like I did.

Sometimes John Morris, a family friend, would take us out in his row boat or drive us to Deep Water. Not many people had boats at the time, so it was always a treat to get to ride in one. John Morris didn't have children of his own and became something of a "town father" in

Montgomery. He was always kind to my siblings and me, taking us out on the boat to go swimming, or buying us treats (including my beloved Butterfingers!). My mother always said that Mr. Morris was so caring and thoughtful that he was certainly headed straight to heaven.

Mr. Morris was there for one of the more memorable moments of my young life—the day I swam across the river. I remember the day well. I had wanted to swim the width of the river for quite a while, and my daddy encouraged my dream. He didn't treat me like some delicate flower because I was a girl; he knew I had an adventurous spirit and didn't try to squash that. Instead, he prepared me for the distance and the river's current by having me swim around a log in the water. Once I could pass the log test, I was ready to take on the river.

The Kanawha River is no trickling stream. It's a branch of the Ohio River and carries a *lot* of water at a fast pace. I knew what I was getting into but, even so, that swim across the river felt *very* long. My daddy and John Morris kept pace beside me in the row boat, shouting encouragements as I swam. My arms and legs grew tired, but I persisted. Stroke after stroke. Kick after kick.

When I reached the other side, I remember the huge grin plastered across my daddy's face. He could not have been prouder.

My mother also supported her children's adventurous undertakings, but she had her limit. One day, some of my friends and I were mountain climbing, jumping from rock to rock. Now, that doesn't sound so bad until you realize that we were several dozen feet high, leaping from one cliff to the other, crossing a gap that was about as wide as a doorway. The sheer drop would have been deadly for any of us if we would have missed our mark and fallen.

My mother was sitting on our front porch and spotted us participating in this perilous game, and our fun came to a quick halt. Needless to say, that was the end of my cliff-jumping days…but it didn't stop me from climbing the trees in our yard or scaling our home's roof.

My brother, Charles Rea, was also quite the trouble-maker and was constantly causing mischief, challenging authority, or running off. Because of his tenaciousness, he became well-acquainted with our mother's Tree of Heaven switches. The Tree of Heaven was a willowy tree with delicate branches that stretched toward the sky. One time, Charles Rea was late coming home and my mother was running around looking for him, worried sick. Finally, she spotted him at the other end of the street and started to run toward him, half-relieved, half-angry.

When he spotted Mother streaming toward him, little Charles Rea scampered to the side of the road, picked up a small branch from the Tree of Heaven, and began swatting himself on the legs in punishment. Of course, my mother couldn't help but laugh and her anger instantly melted away.

GENEROSITY

Be doers of the word and not hearers only.
James 1:22

Getting switched across the legs was completely normal at the time (something that might horrify modern-day parents!), but my parents were never overly-harsh to us. In fact, quite the opposite. They were some of the most kind-hearted, giving people I have ever known.

My siblings and I knew that we could always bring our friends over for dinner and my parents would provide them food without complaint. As I mentioned, we weren't wealthy, but we got by well enough, and our dinner table was always full.

It was so important to my parents to share with those in need that my mother frequently fed the hobos who disembarked at the nearby train station. After feeding a few hungry drifters, it wasn't long before transient men began showing up at our doorstep all the time, looking for a meal! My mother believed our home had been marked as a safe haven, which is why so many men began to appear at our door. Hobos had their own secret code at that time—ways of marking whether a home was safe, friendly, had vicious dogs, or any number of things. My parents never turned a single hungry traveler away.

They were also kind enough to temporarily employ a man every summer who suffered from epileptic seizures and was unable to hold a full-time job. Like the hobos, he was transient and would show up each summer for a few months before hitting the road again. He helped with construction projects, tending the yard, or any other odd job my parents would give him. At night, he slept in our outdoor shed, which was used as both a storage unit and our playhouse.

My parents trusted this man, as they did everyone, but one summer he broke that trust by bringing a woman back to the outdoor shed. That was too much for my parents to tolerate, and they had to make the difficult decision to kick him out.

Most of the time, however, my parents' faith in humanity was justified. They welcomed all kinds of diverse and fascinating people into our home who would tell us stories and expose us to strange and exotic worlds outside of our own little valley. Most people were simply grateful for a hot meal and a temporary escape from the elements.

In 1937 during my freshman year, two young men, Rex and Bernie Chandler (who were related to my friend, George Anderson, who was smitten with me), arrived in Montgomery after a huge flood in Huntington, West Virginia left their family home flooded. This infamous flood was the worst ever recorded in local history. Several dams burst and water rose to more than *nineteen feet* above the flood stage. Thousands of families, including the Chandlers, were displaced, and the town of Montgomery opened its doors to many of those people, doing our best to help with whatever we could.

George's mother, Crystal Anderson, lived in Montgomery, so Rex and Bernie (her brothers) ended up staying with the Andersons. In a small town like Montgomery, everybody knows everybody else, and it wasn't long before I was introduced to Rex and Bernie. After the flood was over, the two young men returned to Huntington, but they continued to keep in touch and both regularly wrote me love letters. They were the mushiest, most sentimental stuff you'd ever read, but I gobbled them up!

In the meantime, I was becoming close friends with George, and we would sometimes even hold hands during church when we thought no one was watching. Unfortunately, George and I lived on different sides of the county line and he had to attend East Bank High, while I attended Montgomery High School. In fact, both the Mason-Dixon Line *and* the county line ran right through the middle of town. Sometimes families that lived a block apart had to send their children to different schools.

That didn't stop us from spending time together. However, I always thought of George as more of a close friend than a boyfriend. I knew he had feelings for me (and, once I started dating other people he promised to "always wait for me," a sentiment that didn't last terribly long!), but I could never truly return those same feelings.

Isn't wasn't long, however, before the tables were turned and *I* began to care about someone who didn't return my feelings. Carl Hammond suddenly entered my life when he rolled into Montgomery during my sophomore year of high school. It was Christmas morning when Jane encountered Carl, sitting on a low wall at a street corner, looking out-of-place and unsure of himself. She approached him and said, "Merry Christmas."

"Merry Christmas," he replied. "Are you having a nice celebration at your house?"

"Yes," Jane said. "With five kids, you have a lot of Christmas."

"That's what I'd be having if I were at home," Carl answered.

"Where's home?"

"Finley, Ohio."

Jane was immediately struck by the fact that Carl had nowhere to go on Christmas and offered, "Why don't you come down and eat with us. My parents won't mind."

And they didn't. In fact, we were all immediately taken with Carl and appreciated his company. He had a lovely tenor voice and joined us that evening in singing with the family while Jane played the piano.

That was the beginning of my long, doe-eyed crush on Carl who, to my delight, stuck around Montgomery and began to drive a laundry service truck (wouldn't it be nice to have someone pick up your dirty clothes, wash them, press them, and return them to your home, neatly folded?). I saw a lot of Carl and used any possible excuse to be by his side.

As many young people can attest, growing up can have its challenges, especially when it comes to young love. I was interested in a couple of boys my age, but they all seemed to be infatuated with other girls. The guys I liked often treated me like a sister and would even use me as a means to connect with the girl they *actually* had a crush on. Unfortunately, this included Carl. He didn't use me as a way to cozy up to other girls, but he did treat me like a sister…and that was tough to swallow.

I admired Carl because he was fearless, full of adventure, and experienced in the world. He had wanted to go to college, but had loaned all of the money he had saved to his sister, who was older and wanted to attend Ohio State University. Unfortunately, the sister got married while still in school, never graduated, and did not have the money to pay back Carl's loan. Frustrated and broke, Carl had no choice but to forgo college. Instead, he took a southbound train, determined to carve out his fortune in a new state, among new people.

In addition to driving the laundry truck, Carl worked for one of the vendors in town called the "Jewel T" man. Jewel T was a company that offered a hodge-podge of home goods such as plates, glasses, and pitchers. They also sold foodstuffs, like tea and coffee. I remember my mother purchasing a set of plates from Carl; they were ringed with an intricate pattern of autumn leaves, which I thought was lovely at the time.

I admired how hard Carl worked and how fearlessly independent he was. Not only that, he was kind and easy to talk to. It was no wonder I began to consider him a yardstick against which I measured all other boys. They had to match Carl's humor, sense of adventure, good looks, and beautiful singing voice, or I wasn't interested.

MUSIC

In those days, one of our simple pleasures was music. When my parents were not working or managing the household, they loved gathering us together and singing—either on the porch or around the piano.

Jane became an accomplished pianist and was the only one who could play music by ear. You could request nearly any song, and Jane would quickly figure out how to play it. It was that astounding talent for music that led her to eventually host her own radio program in Bluefield, West Virginia called "The Voice in the Old Village Choir." Her singing ranged from soothing alto to trilling soprano—always accompanied by her flawless piano-playing—and she would sing everything from hymns to folk music. Sometimes, listeners would call in and request a song, and Jane never let them down.

And it all started around that old piano, or with the seven of us sprawled across our front porch. We sang so often and so well that the next door neighbors, who rented out an apartment over their garage, said they ought to charge their tenants extra for the opportunity to enjoy our entertainment!

The three Dent girls—Jane, Adrah, and myself—were always singing. We sang while we did the dishes, with one of us washing, one drying, and one putting them away. We all eventually grew to be accomplished singers and would sometimes perform as a trio. I remember going to the Lion's Club or other venues around town and singing in front of the crowd. My alto was perfectly complemented by Adrah's soprano, and Jane did the rest! Her vocal range never failed to impress. In fact, she was so talented that she sometimes did solo work around town. When she was only in sixth or seventh grade, Jane sang at the funeral of one of her classmates. The song was so lovely and haunting, it brought us all to tears.

In addition to singing, I also had an interest in the clarinet. I started playing in the fifth grade band with an instrument my parents bought from a neighbor. I had a knack for playing the woodwind instrument, and earned the spot of "first chair." I liked my clarinet well enough, but I dreamed of someday having a new one. In those days, my parents gave us an allowance of ten cents each week, which seemed like a good deal of money at the time! Instead of spending my ten cents on candy or snacks, I usually saved it. In fact, I often traded it in for Jefferson Nickels, which I collected.

My allowance gradually increased to a quarter, and it took five years before I had accumulated enough money to pay for one half of my clarinet. My parents had offered to pay for the other half, and I eagerly accepted their proposal. I had my eye on a Silver King, and no other model would do. In my high school yearbook, there's a picture of me with the school band. I'm proudly holding my silver clarinet, which is positively *gleaming* next to the other plain black woodwinds.

My other interest was photography, and I saved up in a similar way to get my hands on my very first camera. I collected punch cards from advertisements in the local newspaper and sold them to people around Montgomery. Don't ask me what those punch cards were for, because I haven't a clue! All I knew is that people wanted them and, if you sold enough, you were eligible for a brand new, powder blue Kodak camera. With camera in hand, I documented life around Montgomery with fervent enthusiasm. Many of the photographs at the end of this book, in fact, were taken with that very camera.

I also contributed photos to my high school yearbook, as I was on the yearbook committee (and quite eager about it!). My graduating class was actually the first class in our school to put together a high school yearbook. We were also the first class to surpass one-hundred students *and* the first class to have a drum and bugle corps. I'm happy I graduated when I did, and not one year earlier!

CHURCH

My sister, Adrah, had one specific musical ambition. Her goal was to play the organ in the Montgomery Baptist church. The reason she was so determined was because my family had contributed to the purchase of that organ with money we were allotted from the government for my daddy's military service. All veterans were paid a severance and, instead of spending that money on new clothes or house projects, my mother insisted on paying ten-percent of Daddy's bonus to the church for the organ that they so desperately wanted.

She was a firm believer in contributing ten-percent of our family's earning to the church as a tithing. No matter if we were feeling the squeeze of the Great Depression, my family would set aside money each week and put it in the collection basket when it was passed. I remember the envelopes they gave us in which you could choose where to contribute money. Each week, we'd give a small portion to church missions and a larger portion to the church's everyday budget.

I remember seeing that electronic organ and being proud that my family had helped to provide it for the Baptist church. Adrah was proud too, and she talked and talked of one day sitting at the organ and playing for the congregation. Unfortunately, she never got her chance.

My mother, being the pious and industrious woman she was, volunteered as the church secretary. She would attend all the committee meetings and take down the minutes with a quick and accurate hand. The church preacher always attended the meetings and, after a while, my mother could sense that he wasn't entirely trustworthy. One day, he said some inaccurate things to the committee. Then he paused, turned to my mother, and asked her to read back her minutes. She obeyed, reading back every word he had just uttered.

"You're going to have to correct those minutes," the preacher said. "We can't have all that on record."

But my mother refused. To her, lying was one of the worst things a person can do, *especially* a preacher. She promptly stepped down as church secretary and decided to seek a new church.

I can imagine it was a difficult decision for my mother to turn her back on the Baptist church—a church she and her family had attended ever since she could remember—but her principles were strong and she was more loyal to high morals than to a particular branch of Christianity.

My family went along with Mother's convictions and joined the Methodist church, the church in which my daddy was raised. Everyone in my family was fine with making the switch. Everyone, that is, but me.

I was a freshman in college at the time, and I felt attached to the Baptist church and the other parishioners. I stubbornly decided to hold out and stick with the one church I had known my whole life. It wasn't long, however, until I changed my tune…all because of an emergency appendectomy.

I remember the sharp pain in my side. I was rushed to the hospital by ambulance and immediately carted into an operating room. After a successful surgery, I needed time to mend and stayed in the hospital for a few days. None of my Baptist friends came to visit. While that saddened me, I was pleasantly surprised by the handful of Methodist classmates that stopped in to see how I was doing.

Even the Methodist preacher paid me a visit. He was young and full of energy, enthusiastic about God's work. He sat by my bedside and we talked for what felt like quite a long time. In the end, I could see that the Methodist belief system aligned almost perfectly with my own, particularly the belief that a person must accept and claim their own religion, rather than simply be baptized into it.

To this day, I am still a devout Methodist.

After I was released from the hospital, I started attending the Methodist church and began to connect with some of the young people who attended it. After church, we would get together in gatherings dubbed "After Meetings." My family always did love filling our house with people, so it's no surprise that we often hosted the After Meetings. During one such meeting, a young man showed up who had just arrived in town that day. He caught my eye and we started to talk. That young man's name was Jacob Baxter.

Part II

Jake Baxter

A NEW BOY IN TOWN

It was Jake's first night in town. He had left his family's farm in Proctor, West Virginia and driven four or five hours south with his sister, Wilma, to Montgomery in order to start taking classes at the New River State college (later named West Virginia Institute of Technology). He found the Methodist church right away and knew it would be a great place to start making connections and meeting people his age. Churches were the main hubs of activity at the time, and always welcomed new people.

Every Sunday, those youth in our congregation who had attended church that evening were eligible to go to the After Meeting. It was always a fun time, with fifteen or twenty high school and college-aged kids crammed into someone's house (usually ours!). We would have watermelon seed-spitting competitions, make fake teeth out of melon rinds, sing together, and just talk. I remember those times being filled with camaraderie, light-hearted laughter, and some not-too-subtle flirting.

When the After Meetings drew to a close, the boys would split into two groups and walk the ladies home. Half of them escorted the girls who lived in the "lower end" and the other half escorted the "uptown" girls.

When I first met Jake, I was immediately struck by his kind, gentle personality and sense of humor. I was a sophomore in high school at the time, and still crazy about Carl, but a part of my heart opened to this young stranger. He was interested in someone else at the time too—a little redhead from his hometown—so we started off simply as friends.

Over time, however, we stopped thinking about our other love interests and realized we only had eyes for each other.

It was a slow evolution. We fell into an easy friendship, filled with After Meetings and long talks. Then, Jake started working and living at the Woman's Club House just across the alley from our house while continuing his college education. He did janitorial and maintenance work at the Club in exchange for lodging in the basement. One day, I invited him to our house for breakfast and, after that, he showed up every morning like clockwork. Those breakfasts with my family were the start of something deeper—the blossoming of true, everlasting love.

MONTGOMERY COLLEGE

Do your best to present yourself to God as one proved.
A workman who has no need to be ashamed.
2 Timothy 2:15

While I was finishing high school and Jake was earning his degree in Industrial Arts, we continued to see other people, but my heart wasn't truly in it. I went to the East Bank High School prom with George Anderson, and tried to make it clear that we were just going as friends.

For my own high school prom, my friends and I didn't have dates, but instead met as a group. I remember Carl (of all people!) drove me to prom and dropped me off at the door…just like an older brother would do for his sister.

My mother made my prom dress, as she did all our clothes, and I remember feeling lovely wearing it. It was ankle-length and light in color—dotted Swiss with light blue accents. The sleeves were slightly puffed and it had a low collar with a long bow down the front.

Even though I didn't go to prom with Jake, I had strong feelings for him and was growing more attached to him by the day. In my high school yearbook under the "Likes" section, my friends wrote: Carl, John, and Jake! That may have been true at the time, but it wasn't long before I *only* had eyes for Jake.

After high school graduation, Jake and I shared one year at West Virginia Institute of Technology (WVIT) together before he completed his undergrad degree, joined the Civil Service, and moved away to work at Chanute Air Force Base in Rantoul, Illinois.

College was a new and exciting adventure for me. Even though I still lived at home, I *felt* different. I was an adult now, just as serious about my studies as I was about having fun.

My parents valued a good education and encouraged all of the Dent children to pursue a college degree. The only one who rebelled was Jane, who was determined to get married and settle down with a nice young man. As usual, Jane achieved her goal! She married Howard Meadows at the age of seventeen when she was a senior in high school and he was in his second year of college.

I, on the other hand, wouldn't have missed college for the world. Since my family was not wealthy enough to pay for schooling outright, I worked a few different jobs to pay for tuition, in addition to receiving a small loan of $300 from the Women's Auxiliary, which I was able to pay off just one year after graduation.

There were two movie theaters in town, the Avalon and the Kayton—both owned by Mr. McKay—and I alternated working at each of them as a cashier. I was paid twenty-five cents per hour at first, until I became head cashier and earned a ten cent raise. My friend, James, worked the popcorn station at the theater, and we nicknamed him Jolly Time Kid, after the brand of popcorn.

Sitting in the cramped booth, I wasn't allowed to read or do much of anything besides take in money and hand out tickets. However, with World War II ramping up and more and more American boys heading overseas, I *was* allowed to knit for the troops. Like my mother and sisters, I enjoyed needlework—knitting, tatting, sewing…you name it! I made scarves, socks, wrist bands, gloves, and ski masks for our troops, who were often ill-prepared to face the winter cold in northern Europe. The Red Cross furnished the wool yarn – khaki for the Army and dark blue for the Navy.

In addition to my *glamorous* cashier job, I also worked for the junior high principal, Doyle Wickline (who had been my second grade teacher), cutting stencils that were used for printing. These were the days before copying machines and even before printing presses were widespread. If you wanted to make a copy of something, you used a ditto machine or a mimeograph. The ditto machine involved typing the letters of your text in a specific purple ink and transferring them onto a special paper. Using hand pressure, the ink was transferred to the paper copy—a lot of work to copy a single page! For mimeograph, you typed a stencil sheet which was then put on an inked drum and, by turning the handle of the drum, ink was transferred to paper fed through the machine. The mimeograph method was still used when I worked at our church in the 1960s. Later, we would use the Xerox or copy machines we have today.

When I wasn't working at the two theaters or cutting stencils, I also babysat for families around town. I was paid twenty-five cents an hour…unless the couple came home after midnight. After that, my rate doubled to fifty cents per hour!

All this work was, of course, in addition to my college classes. I was a good student and did well in most classes, with the exception of two: accounting and mining studies. My accounting class was taught by a lewd man who gave preferential treatment to certain girls—the types who wore low-cut dresses and would flirt with him after class. I refused to fall into that kind of behavior and dreaded going to my accounting class, which is probably why I didn't do as well as I could have.

Mining studies (which focused on mining methods, discovery of ores, and how to look for places to mine coal) was just plain difficult. I took it as an elective and it quickly became clear that I was not cut out for the class. Many of the students came from mining families and were already familiar with the terminology and techniques the professor taught. I struggled to keep up and, to my horror, started to fail the class. WVIT was a small school—only about 350 students—and the faculty cared about the success of each and every one of us. That's why my failing grade was noticed by the dean, and he eventually called me to his office and asked if I wanted to drop the class. I gladly agreed, and that was the end of my brief study of the mining industry!

My interests, like my mother's, were more aligned with teaching. I majored in secretarial teacher training and became proficient at typing, shorthand, and salesmanship in order to teach these skills to others. I enjoyed the work and did my practice teaching at Montgomery High School. The students were only a few years younger than I—and many of them were friends with my younger siblings—so they had a hard time calling me "Miss Dent." Besides, I didn't really feel like a "Miss Dent" at the time. Despite all my many responsibilities and jobs, I was still young and loved to have fun.

COLLEGE LIFE

Almost all the female students at WVIT were in one of the school's three sororities. I decided to join the girls in Sigma Iota Chi (Sigmas, for short), and they quickly became like sisters to me. We were a group of less than twenty and spent our time playing sports, planning events, running for school office positions, and simply keeping each other company and offering support.

In a mostly co-ed school, it's essential to have this kind of network—a group of girls that will offer help and advice on everything from math exams to relationships. I'm sure we also did some community work, but to be honest, I mostly remember all the fun we had.

Even initiation was fun, in a way. As Pledges, we had to do all kinds of things like crazy dress-ups, wearing oil in our hair, or collecting signatures on a paddle from professors. And (oh, yes!) there was the paddle. The paddle was a flat, wooden board that became infamous in our sorority. During initiation, every "Active" had to make a checkmark on the paddle next to her name every day, or the Pledge would be smacked on the behind with the paddle. The Active members also used the paddle during the question/answer sessions they held with each recruit. An unsatisfactory answer resulted in a swat with the paddle.

When my mother caught wind of this activity, she gave me strict instructions to not let the girls hit me. I had just had my appendix removed and who *knows* what a whack with the paddle might do! So, when I went in for my question/answer session, I was ready. The girls began to ask me all kinds of embarrassing and outlandish questions, and I told them exactly what they wanted to hear…until they tripped me up with a question that, in my mind, crossed the line.

"Did Jake ever tell you he loved you?" one of the girls asked.

I scoffed at the girl and straightened my shoulders. "I don't think it's any of your business," I said.

"Okay," the girl replied with a smug grin. "It's the paddle for you, then."

"I don't think so," I said. My feistiness was taking over and I refused to be intimidated by the Actives. "I've just had my appendix removed and you *cannot* give me a paddling."

I must have convinced them because they grudgingly put the paddle aside and, despite my impudence, I was still allowed to join the sorority.

After initiation, most of the Sigmas' activities were pure fun, and far more harmless. We had a basketball team and competed with other local schools. These were the early days of women in sports, so we still had to look *somewhat* ladylike while we played. That meant our uniforms did not consist of shorts and t-shirts, but rather a button-down sleeveless top that connected to a pair of puffy bloomers! Our outfits would seem ridiculous by today's standards and, even then, I thought they were hideous. But that was the uniform, and what choice did I have?

The rules for women's basketball only allowed three dribbles to advance the ball before a pass or a shot. There were two guards and three forwards on each team, and they had to remain on their side of the center line. They could not cross to the other side of the court. Apparently, women were not thought to have the same stamina as men!

In warm weather, the Sigmas would get together and participate in outdoor activities. We were always busy playing volleyball or tennis, going on picnics, or swimming. Since the girls were outnumbered at least five to one by college boys, it wasn't unusual to bump into groups of guys who were also outside, taking advantage of the warm weather that was typical from about April to October. But the guys liked their privacy at times and would steal off to places where the girls usually wouldn't venture. One of those places was the top of the town water tower.

At the time, Montgomery was hosting both the Signal Corps boys and the Civilian Conservation Corps (CCC) workers—both of whom were groups of unmarried young men, ages 18 – 25, who were working in a work-relief program. This Depression-era program provided unskilled manual jobs related to conservation and development of natural resources in rural lands owned by the government. It was the Signal Corps boys who usually liked to climb the tower, and we wondered what they were up to and why they never invited us to join them. Well, I decided to take matters into my own hands and find out.

One day, we spotted some Signal Corps boys climbing up the narrow water tower ladder. Being the fearless young lady that I was, I volunteered to climb up after them. The rungs of the ladder were worn and slippery; the angle was steep. I didn't look down as I climbed up, up…

The surprise at the top of the water tower was terribly disappointing. The Signal Corps boys were only lounging around, soaking in the last rays of the autumn sun. I had climbed all that way just to discover they'd been doing nothing but sunbathing!

Although I had always been an adventurous tomboy, I still enjoyed dressing up and participating in some of the more ladylike activities at the school, including homecoming. During my second year of college, my sorority sister, Helene Whitt, was chosen to be the homecoming queen and I was in her court. This was one of many dances the school held throughout the year, and they were always filled with fun, laughter, and the sparks of romance you'd expect to find among love-crazy young people. Jake and I were usually student chaperones due to the fact that we did not consume alcohol (what we call "designated drivers" today!)

We all wore long dresses (many of them homemade) that usually had gathered sleeves and a few small embellishments, such as bows or buttons. Throughout my college years, I attended school dances with a few different dates at my side, but I wasn't serious about any of them, except Jake Baxter. What started with daily breakfasts and friendship, had evolved into a love that was strong enough to withstand two years and several hundred miles of separation.

During my second year of college, Jake was working with the Civil Service, where he taught air force cadets the mechanics of airplane motors. Despite the distance, we were determined to keep in touch. He wrote me a letter *every single day*. I would bring my unopened letter to the dinner table and my daddy would tease me, saying, "She can't eat yet. She's got to have her dessert first!"

My family finally had a radio during this time and every Sunday night we would listen to Phil Spitalny and his "All Girls Orchestra." Jake and I had a deal where we would each listen to the program and then he would call me. Our phone calls were limited to once a week because the long distance rates were very costly at that time. It was part of our weekly routine—the letters, listening to Phil Spitalny, talking with each other on the phone. We were becoming deeply entrenched in each other's lives and we both knew that someday we would be married.

I NOW PRONOUNCE YOU...

It was during my third year at WVIT that Jake popped the question. The moment didn't exactly come as a surprise, as we knew we cared about one another and had already discussed getting married. I remember Jake had borrowed a friend's car, and we drove around a little while before he stopped the car and turned to me, saying, "You know, I really love you."

I shot him a sly smile. "I love you too, I think."

"Will you marry me?"

"Well," I said, ever the strong personality, "I have to finish college first."

Jake laughed and agreed. He knew college was important to me and fully supported my decision.

And that was that. Jake slipped a ring on my finger—an engagement ring that would eventually match my wedding ring. It had a plain gold band with a small, circular diamond on top. He had purchased the ring in Champaign, with the help of his friend who owned Reed's Jewelry Store. Though it was a simple ring, that tiny diamond held worlds of hope and promise inside its pale core.

I was determined to graduate from college before marrying Jake, as I promised my parents I would, but I didn't wait terribly long after my diploma was in hand. I graduated on a Friday and was married that Sunday!

I was the first of my family to graduate with a college degree. Adrah was next, with a degree in religious education from Scarritt College and WVIT. Morris then attended Marshall College, where he met his wife, Eleanor. They moved to Champaign where he graduated from the University of Illinois in mathematics. Charles Rea attended West Virginia Wesleyan, where he acquired both a degree in music and a wife, Mary Beth. Morris served in the Marine Corps and Charles Rea served in the Air Force, and both used the G.I. Bill to attend college. The G.I. Bill was a blessing to many veterans at the time, as it granted stipends that covered tuition and expenses for colleges or trade schools.

Even though Jake and I decided to have a modest wedding, I was still thrilled by all the preparations and excitement around the event. The days leading up to July 18, 1943 included a shopping trip to Charleston, a wedding shower, and plenty of planning. We were having a wartime wedding, which meant there wasn't a lot of room for frivolity, but it was still *our* wedding.

My mother and I made a trip to Diamonds Department Store in Charleston, where we purchased my wedding dress. The wedding dress was simple and elegant. It was a two-piece outfit with a skirt that reached mid-calf and a jacket with elbow-length sleeves. By today's standards, it hardly looked like a wedding dress—no lace, no chiffon, no bustle—but I felt like a queen when I wore it. I decided to pair it with gloves and a smart-looking hat, which had pleats in front and a short veil in the back that could be removed so I could reuse the hat. The flowers were provided by the florist shop owned by my Uncle George Miller's wife, Miss Ora.

My wedding shower was meant to be a surprise, thrown by the women from our church. However, one of our neighbors ended up accidentally spilling the beans when she told me how sorry she was that she couldn't make it. I remember grinning from ear-to-ear when I found out I'd be having a shower, and it did *not* disappoint.

Though many people at the time were not well off, everyone brought me a thoughtful gift, whether handmade or purchased from a store. I had only registered for one thing—a set of silverware in a pattern called "courtship"—and I ended up getting the entire set, a few items at a time. One guest might give me a fork, another a knife. I remember one of Jake's professors, Mr. Grove, gave me a single spoon from the collection and also made me a lovely little silver pickle fork.

I was overwhelmed by the incredible generosity of my community. By the end of the shower, I had received sets of sheets, serving dishes, cookware, a glass tea kettle, pillow cases with hand-tatted trim from Jane, a Pyrex casserole dish from Morris and two of his friends, and many other useful items that I could use to start a new life—and a new home—with Jake.

One of my most treasured gifts from that day was a cookbook compiled by the women of the Montgomery Woman's Club and presented to me by Mrs. Macklin. She included little notes next to many of the recipes, telling me which ones were filling, simple to make, or good for a sweet tooth. I have made many recipes from this little cookbook and still use it from time to time, always smiling when I open it and see Mrs. Macklin's little notes.

Not long after my shower, the big day arrived. With preparations complete and a college degree acquired, I was ready to begin a new life with Jacob Baxter.

It was a warm July morning. Sunlight filtered past the trees and radiated through the stained glass windows of Montgomery Methodist Church. The most important people in our lives were gathered together in the wooden pews, their smiles beaming as brightly as the eight a.m. sunshine. My family, my soon-to-be sister-in-law, Wilma, and a church filled with friends joined us that morning to give their blessings and wish us well.

Before my daddy walked me down the aisle, he leaned over to me—always the joker—and said, "When the preacher asks, 'Who gives this woman in marriage,' I'll say, 'I do, gladly!'" It wasn't that he wanted me out of the house, it was that he could see the writing on the wall far earlier than I could. He and my mother both knew that Jake and I would end up together.

My sister, Adrah, was my maid of honor, and Jane's husband (and Jake's good friend), Howard Meadows, was the best man.

I walked down the aisle to the melodic tones of the organ played by my Aunt Lillian's best friend, Miss Virginia Newby. Waiting for me at the altar, dressed in a dark grey suit and a figured tie with maroon background, was my husband-to-be, smiling at me as if it were the first time he had ever laid eyes on me. I just beamed up at Jake.

It was one of the happiest days of my life and I knew, with certainty, that God had brought us together to start a new chapter of our lives. Even though Jake was far too young when he left this earth, I still know that we were meant to spend our young adult lives together, side by side.

OUR "HONEYMOON"

After our wedding, we didn't linger long in Montgomery. We hopped on the number three train to Huntington, West Virginia, a stopover on our way to the Baxter Farm. I wore the traveling dress that my mother had made especially for the trip. I loved that dress with its pleated beige linen skirt and hand-embroidered pockets. My purse in one hand and my new husband's hand in the other, I stepped onto the train as friends and relatives showered us with rice.

When we got on the train, we realized it was so full that there were not two empty seats together. I sat down and, fortunately, the man in the seat next to me had noticed the rice-throwing. He commented on the rice on my clothing and in Jake's hair and asked if Jake was my groom. When I confirmed that he was, the man said, "Far be it for me to be the first man to separate the two of you!" He got up and changed seats with Jake. Later, a group of sailors on the train went to the dining car and brought back a vase with a tiger lily in it to set in our window. I am often humbled and amazed by the kindness of strangers.

Jake and I spent one night together in Huntington before continuing on to the Baxter Farm, where we would spend the rest of our time off together. Today, not many people would consider this trip a honeymoon, but that's what it was to us! It didn't matter that we were staying with Jake's family in a house that didn't yet have electricity or indoor plumbing—we were blissfully happy.

The property where Jake grew up was owned by his grandparents, the Smiths. The property consisted of a large hill with two homes. One was located at the top of the hill (called the House on the Hill) and another home was at the bottom of the hill near Proctor Creek. They also owned land across the creek which was used for farming and grazing animals.

Growing up, Jake's father (Herman Baxter) and their family lived with Herman's brother (Woolsey Baxter) and his family in the House on the Hill. Herman and Woolsey had married sisters—Josephine and Pearl Bohrer, respectively—and the families were quite close. Both couples had six children each, and little Jake swore that babies were simply delivered to one's house in black satchels!

Herman and Woolsey's sister, Sample, lived in the house near the creek along with Grandma Smith. Upon her death, Grandma Smith divided the property in half. Woolsey and his family remained in the House on the Hill and Herman's family moved down to the house near the creek.

I remember the House on the Hill well. The kitchen was in a separate building attached to the house; the stove was a massive cast iron appliance that filled most of the space. To heat the stovetop, we had to fill the belly of the stove with wood, light a fire, and wait for it to reach the right temperature. Each end of the stove contained bins with water, which could also be heated by the fire. Above the stove, a shelf acted as a warming plate, as the heat from the fire would rise and keep whatever was sitting on it relatively warm. It was a clever instrument that was capable of cooking for a crowd, but it was difficult to master, and hot as the dickens when you were near it!

My mother-in-law, Josephine, kept a large garden and could often be found pickling or canning when she was not cooking or baking her delicious bread. The families only grew a few crops on their land, however. The bulk of their faming was carried out on land they rented near New Martinsville, West Virginia. Most of the crops the family grew were meant for their livestock. They kept cows and donkeys on their property across the creek and they all had to pitch in to tend them. I remember being fascinated by Wilma's stories of herding the animals across the river in the morning on her way to teach in a one-room schoolhouse. The donkeys and cows would graze during the day in the field, and on her way home, Wilma would round them up and take them back across the creek to the big red barn that still stands on the property.

After Jake and I were married, I grew to love the Baxter family and their simple home more and more with each passing year. Even though I had to get used to some household quirks like gas lamps, an outhouse, and a hand pump for cold water (only!) at the kitchen sink, it was always warm and welcoming inside that farmhouse, even if it *was* crowded when all the Baxter children were at home! Jake was the middle child of five surviving children (one had died in infancy). Ralph and Wilma were older, Faye and George younger. By the time we arrived at the farmhouse for our honeymoon, Ralph and Faye were already married. Faye, in fact, had been married since the tender age of sixteen and eventually ended up getting a divorce at age thirty—an act that was quite rare at the time. George would marry in 1947 and Wilma in 1949.

On the first night of our honeymoon, we were greeted by the loud clatter of pots and pans banging outside our bedroom window. Jake laughed, knowing immediately what was happening, but I was puzzled. He explained that this was a regional tradition called shivaree. The local children would band together and make noise outside the window of a newlywed couple's bedroom in an effort to interrupt. They would also leave cans of food on the doorstep and cause other mischief. The tradition is thought to bring good luck, so we just smiled and endured the interruptions.

During our week-long honeymoon with the Baxters, I had a second wedding shower with their family. My father-in-law decided to get us a practical gift and took us to the local Proctor grocery store so we could pick out a nice butcher knife. You have to admire the quality of goods from that time—the knife has held up wonderfully, and I still use it to this day.

Although most of our honeymoon was filled with joy and peaceful family gatherings, one black smudge marred our stay. We were invited by Jake's Aunt Sample to have dinner at her home at the bottom of the hill. While the dinner was lovely (Aunt Sample was an excellent cook), the post-dinner talk was anything *but* lovely. The Baxters were members of the Church of God and Aunt Sample was a devout follower and a preacher in the church. I remember gathering on the porch after dinner and having her lay into me about the "bad thing I did by bringing Jake into the Methodist church." She admonished me for my religion and said that the only worthy branch of Christianity was the Church of God.

During her preaching, Jake's father paced the yard, looking increasingly uncomfortable. The others remained quiet, their eyes turned away from Aunt Sample and me. And as for me—my cheeks burned, partly from embarrassment, partly from fury. I had to say something to defend myself, so I chose my words carefully, saying, "Aunt Sample, Methodism is the religion of my entire family…and we're all still very active in the church."

That caught her off-guard and she was quiet for a little while. You see, some of her other family had left the Church of God, thinking it too overbearing on their lives. During her moment of silence, Herman saw his opportunity to jump in and say, "Okay, I think that's enough. We'd better be going."

Needless to say, that was the last time we ever received a dinner invitation from Aunt Sample!

It just goes to show you that country life isn't necessarily idyllic. It must be human nature to stir up drama. Lord knows, the Baxters had their share of it! For years, they had been engaged in a feud with a nearby family called the Newmans. Nobody ever explained to me how the fight began, but one of the Newman men ended up shooting Jake's grandfather (Herman and Woolsey's father) to death while he was on his front porch. After that, a line was drawn. The two families hated each other.

After Uncle Woolsey died, his wife, Pearl, was eventually remarried...to a Newman! Needless to say, Herman was furious and would not allow Mr. Newman onto Baxter land. If Pearl wanted to visit Grandma Baxter, Mr. Newman would have to drop her off at the property line and then pick her up later. He would not allow that man to step one toe onto Baxter property.

It was hard for me to reconcile the friendly man I knew as Jake's father with the cold and calloused man he could become in the face of the Newmans. To me, Herman Baxter was always kind, generous, and a wonderful family man. I enjoyed spending time with Herman and the rest of the Baxter clan over summer vacations or during the Christmas holiday, which was always a lot of fun since the house was positively packed with Baxter children and their families.

For Christmas, it was tradition to draw names from a hat and purchase one present for whomever you drew. That was how I accidentally started a cup and saucer collection! Ralph and Edith had drawn my name and purchased a lovely cup and saucer set that depicted a detailed landscape with hand-painted trees and flowers in the foreground and a mountainside lake in the background. Attached to the gift was a note: "For your collection."

I didn't have a collection, so I was puzzled, but graciously accepted the gift. It turns out, Wilma was actually the one with the cup and saucer collection, but I saw it as an opportunity to start a collection of my own. Since then, I have acquired over twenty cup and saucer sets, and each one has its own unique story. This collection has been divided between my granddaughter, Samantha, and my grandson Derek's wife, Stacy.

ADVENTURES IN NEW HAVEN

Immediately after our honeymoon stay with the Baxters, we took a northbound train to New Haven, Connecticut, home of Yale University. The Civil Service, where Jake worked at Chanute Field in Illinois, had expanded, spreading its bases of operation to Connecticut, North Carolina, and Arizona. Jake chose to go to New Haven, where he would continue doing the same kind of work—teaching cadets about airplane engines—but in the glamour of an Ivy League school.

Jake and his fellow instructors did a lot of hands-on work with airplanes and required actual engines to demonstrate various components and maintenance or repair techniques to their students. Because of that, many of the demo aircraft engines had to be moved from Chanute Field to Yale. These engines were enormous and difficult to maneuver…and they all had to be hauled across the pristine marble floors of Sterling Law Building. Fortunately, not a single marble tile was cracked and the engines made it to Jake's wing of the building without incident.

Having never been to the northeastern part of the country, I was positively filled with excitement. It was all an adventure—a new marriage; a new part of the country; a fresh set of friends, co-workers, and church members. Even though I was far from home, I was—true to form—up for anything!

The next year and a half in New Haven proved to be blissful, as well as busy. I worked as a substitute for various secretaries and took on a handful of typing jobs. I tried to keep busy so I could pay off my college loan *and* maintain a nice household for Jake and myself.

We lived in a little apartment and were frugal by necessity. Not only did we have little money, the war limited our spending power. Those were the days of ration books, and firm restrictions were placed on certain items. We received a book of stamps each month, detailing the quantity of specific goods we could buy: red stamps for meat, blue for canned goods, green for gas, and yellow for shoes. My mother would periodically send us extra red stamps, which I took to the German butcher down the street. I would say to him, "I have this many red stamps and my pan is this big," and he would then select an appropriate cut of meat. For some reason, he also insisted on giving me detailed instructions on how to prepare the meat, even though I already knew how to make the Swiss steak or the roasted chicken that I often cooked.

Jake and I were able to occasionally buy goods without using our stamps, but that was quite rare. On one such occasion, I purchased a pair of shoes without using any of my yellow stamps…but they were close to the consistency and durability of cardboard! These shoes were so flimsy, in fact, that they nearly disintegrated in the rain during a particularly long bike ride.

We didn't have a car in New Haven and often biked around the University, but never more than a few miles. One weekend, however, we decided to accompany two other couples on a twenty-five mile ride through the nearby countryside to a state park. We had planned to stay in the park that evening, but when we arrived, there were no more vacancies. So, we pressed on another two miles to a quaint bed and breakfast.

Though the scenery was lovely, my bike (and my behind!) were not equipped to endure twenty-five miles of steep hills. I was so saddle-sore by the end of the ride that I could barely sit on the edge of the bathtub to soak my feet.

On the way back to New Haven, the skies opened up and it poured. I pedaled hard and prayed that my thin shoes would hold up until we arrived home. They did, barely, and I knew I'd have to use one of next month's yellow stamps for a more durable pair of shoes!

Our next big trip out of New Haven was far less athletic. We decided to join a few other couples on a day trip to New York City. The mere thought of New York excited me, but seeing it took my breath away. I'm sure I walked around like a typical tourist with my neck craned up, taking in the impossibly high buildings and all the gleaming glass and steel. The honking cars, bright yellow taxis, and mobs of people of all ethnicities and backgrounds were overwhelming for someone like me, whose exposure to big cities had been limited to Roanoke, Charleston, and New Haven.

We visited several iconic sites: the Empire State Building, Wall Street (where one of our friends picked up the ticker tape and pretended to read it like a stock broker!), the Chrysler Building, and Radio City Music Hall. It was here, in Radio City Music Hall, that I laid eyes on my very first television set. The TV was small—about the size of a large picture frame—and was, of course, black and white. A video camera had filmed us when we had walked into the building, and then displayed that footage on the television. I was astounded! There I was, in crisp black and white, on the screen. "This is the future," I remember thinking. "I'm seeing it right here in New York City."

Although New York was incredible, we could only afford to go once during our time in New Haven. Most of our adventures were closer to home and involved trips to nearby parks or hosting card nights with Colonel Sparks, Jake's commanding officer. We would also visit nearby Savin Rock Park for softball games or go to Double Beach, which offered swimming, a Ferris wheel, swings, and a few other rides. Most of this entertainment was free, but we'd occasionally treat ourselves to a movie—an indulgence we didn't do terribly often, as we were trying to save our pennies.

Always the sporting type, Jake played softball in a league with some of his co-workers. Even though I would have loved to play too, this league was for men and I'd usually sit in the bleachers with the other wives and watch him play. Every once in a great while, the ladies also had a chance to play alongside their husbands. I never played softball in school, but my daddy had taught me how to swing a bat, so I could hold my own.

One time, one of the wives was drinking a beer and asked me to hold it while she got up to bat. I stood there, eyeing the beer, and had to do everything in my power to resist pouring it onto the ground. Jake and I were strict about alcohol and never touched the stuff. It was a principle that had been passed down to us by our parents. Jake's mother simply believed it went against the church's teaching, and my mother had an aversion to it because of the struggles her father had faced with over-consumption.

Though we never preached about it, we tried to be good role models. We taught Sunday school classes in New Haven, and later, in Champaign, we became counselors for college students. We took our mentoring seriously and tried to live good, clean lives that our students could emulate. I remember going to dinner one time at a nice restaurant and catching a glimpse of the tables. Each table had a bottle of wine as its centerpiece that could be opened if we chose to do so. When I saw that, I was adamant that our bottle be removed. Even though we wouldn't tap into it, there was a chance one of our students would see us with a bottle of wine at our table and think that we had double standards. Living a good, moral life was something my mother had instilled in me from a young age, and I took her lessons seriously.

Rejoice always, pray constantly,
give thanks in all circumstances…
test everything; hold fast to what is good,
abstain from all appearance of evil.
1 Thessalonians 5:16-22

WHEN THE DRAFT CALLS…

Jake shared the same strong sense of morality and always strove to live out his morals. That meant when Uncle Sam came a knockin', he would honor his draft call and go fight in the war. We lived in New Haven from 1943 to 1944, while World War II was raging in both the European and Pacific theaters. During this time, Jake was called upon to take a special Civil Service assignment in the Aleutian Islands—a chain of fourteen large, volcanic islands, and several smaller ones, which sweep out into the Bering Sea from mainland Alaska.

This so-called "Detached Civil Service Assignment" was important to the country, as the Aleutian Islands are not far from Russia and Japan—countries who were then part of the Axis Powers. In fact, the island of Kiska had fallen under control of the Japanese at the time, so Jake was to be sent to the perimeter of dangerous territory. I understood why he was needed, though. The planes flying in and out of the Aleutian Islands were having trouble with their motors freezing up in the cold Alaskan temperatures, so they needed engine mechanics like Jake to assist with maintenance and repairs.

Jake took off on his special assignment, and I decided to go home to Montgomery to be with my family for a while. On the southbound train, I happened to bump into a boy who lived right next door to my parents, as well as a Montgomery Catholic priest. I told the priest about Jake's assignment in the Aleutian Islands (without specifically saying "Aleutian Islands" so as to not disclose his location) and why I was heading home for a little while. Well, he must have wanted to make me feel better about the whole thing, so he bought a piping hot cup of coffee and handed it to me. Though I'm not a coffee drinker, I accepted his kind gesture and, when he wasn't looking, I dashed off, poured it down the sink, and filled it up with water. He must not have suspected a thing, because he later offered to buy me a second cup!

While Jake was in the Aleutians and I was in West Virginia, a little piece of paper came in the mail: a draft notice. I was already anxious about Jake being in the remotest part of Alaska on the edge of the action, but now my anxiety increased tenfold. How could Jake—the gentlest man I'd ever known—suit up and prepare to fight, and potentially kill, other men? Jake, with his even temper and calm disposition, wasn't a fighter; he hardly raised his voice, let alone swung his fists or shot a gun.

I brought the draft notice to the attention of Colonel Sparks, Jake's supervisor. The Colonel, who was a good friend of ours, took one look at the notice and promised he would do everything he could to help. He contacted the Whetzel County Selective Service Board in West Virginia and explained to them that Jake was serving his country in the Aleutian Islands and could not easily return to answer his draft call.

I still remember the wave of relief that passed over me when the Selective Service Board decided to advocate for Jake and request a temporary draft waiver from the U.S. government. The government honored the request, and Jake was safe…for the time being.

After Jake returned from his detached Civil Service assignment in the Aleutian Islands, he was called upon to move once more. The Civil Service operation had consolidated and all operations would once again be based out of Chanute Field in Rantoul, Illinois, just outside the city of Champaign. Jake chose to return to his post at Chanute Field. So, back to the Midwest we went.

Driving from New Haven to Champaign, we decided to stop and see family along the way. One stop was in Moundsville, West Virginia where Jake's Aunt Mary lived. While our loaded car was parked, two little boys peeked into the window and saw the form I used for sewing dresses. I heard one of them shout, "Look! There's a body in there!"

We settled into Champaign, and it wasn't long before we had our first child, Janie. She was born in June, 1945, and two months later we received that dreaded white piece of paper in the mail once more. Another draft notice.

I dutifully started packing, preparing to move back to Montgomery, West Virginia, where I would stay with my young daughter until the end of the war. At some point, we realized that if we removed the back seat of the car and shipped it to West Virginia, we could get all our belongings inside the car.

Back seat shipped, suitcases packed, and car loaded, we were ready to make the trip back to Montgomery when the news struck: VJ Day! Victory in Japan!

The Japanese army had finally surrendered and, after six long years, the war was over. Any men over the age of twenty-six no longer had to report for active duty. On that day of August 14, 1945, we could breathe easily for the first time, knowing that Jake wouldn't be called into service. I thanked God that day, and many days afterward, knowing that He was watching over us and keeping us safe.

The town erupted with celebration on that hot August day, and we joined in the festivities, feeling light as a pair of feathers. At the center of town was an open area called five points, named after the five streets that converged there, and the space filled to the brim with people, laughter, and the blare of live bands.

We moved all of our belongings back into our apartment in Champaign and asked Mother and Daddy to ship the seat back to us!

SETTLING INTO CHAMPAIGN

Before the war's end—and before the narrowly-avoided draft notice—we were just another young couple, settling into a new life with a baby on the way. I had enjoyed New Haven, but I loved Champaign just as much and could easily see us carving out a life there.

We moved to Champaign in a used car we had purchased for somewhere between $150 and $200. We had a few boxes of kitchen supplies, my sewing machine, dress form, and clothing…and that's about it. One of Jake's friends, Mr. Chumley, was a realtor and offered to help us find an apartment. While he was helping us look, Mr. Chumley let us stay in his home for a week. His wife, Mrs. Chumley, was kind, but full of opinions.

"I think all newlywed couples should wait two years to have children," she declared one night. "It's just for the best."

I couldn't help putting a hand to my belly when she said that and thinking about the little life blossoming inside me. I was pregnant with Janie at the time, and couldn't have been more excited, despite Mrs. Chumley's opinion. Jake and I had talked about having several children, and we were both eager to get our family started.

In Champaign, we looked at several apartments before finding one that suited our needs, and the future needs of our child. But, it seemed like everything within our budget was either roach-infested or falling apart. Finally, we found a cozy little apartment located on Hill Street, just behind our Methodist Church. The minister at the time, H. Clifford Northcott, would often climb the three stories of stairs at our back entrance just to see how we were doing. Once we moved in, we began building a new life for ourselves, which included (for me) finding a job and learning how to drive.

I didn't want to strain myself during my first pregnancy, but I knew we needed any extra money I could bring in. With my background in secretarial training, I was able to easily pick up a job as a substitute secretary for an insurance company, a dental office, and the church. I filled in for any secretary who was ill or needed a couple days off. I typed and filed, using any scrap of money I earned to help pay for our expenses.

With a job secured, I started to work toward my other goal: learning how to drive. I had never needed to learn how to drive in the past—most of my travel had been by foot, bicycle, or train. But cars were becoming more and more popular and, since Jake and I now owned one, we both agreed I should learn how to operate it. I practiced driving with Jake at my side, learning how to gently let out the clutch and shift gears. When it became time to take my road test, it was the dead of winter and I was in my second trimester. That day, a horrible mix of snow and freezing rain fell on Champaign, coating the roads with a slick layer of ice.

I took my written test, passed it effortlessly, and then met with a man who facilitated driving tests. He took one look at my pregnant belly, glanced out the window at the freezing rain, and said to Jake, "Can she drive okay?"

"She's a good driver," Jake said. "We've been practicing."

The man nodded. "Okay, then. I'm not about to make a pregnant woman drive in this mess. If you say she's a good driver, she's a good driver. A husband's word is enough in my book."

He then turned to me and said, "I'm giving you a pass."

I'm probably one of the few people who got my driver's license without ever having to take a road test!

BABY JANIE

Spring dawned in Champaign and the air buzzed with excitement. The trees lining the University's sidewalks burst into shades of green, and the University students traded their sweaters and winter boots for short-sleeved shirts and tennis shoes. This would be the first of over *forty* springs in Champaign, a place that I still think of as a second home.

As the due date for our first child approached, Jake and I busied ourselves with preparations and trips to the doctor's office. I liked my new doctor—a man by the name of Dr. Moss—but, unfortunately, he suffered from a stroke and passed away one month before Janie was due. At the last minute, we had to switch to Dr. Guernon, a cold, irritable man who didn't seem to care two licks about me.

On June 2, 1945, our daughter finally arrived. I hadn't been through any of the coaching or classes that are now standard for most mothers today. In fact, I remember complaining to a friend in the grocery store about the stomach cramps I was experiencing every few minutes. The friend raised an eyebrow and said, "Are you sure they're cramps?"

Sure enough, they were contractions. I rushed home and tried to stay calm. It was just after noon and I knew Jake wouldn't be home until three o'clock, so I called my friend, Emmy, and asked her to take me to the hospital. Just as we were heading out the door, Jake arrived and we all went to the hospital together. Jake and Emmy were not allowed in the room while I was giving birth, but they waited out in the lobby while I delivered our first child. This is VERY different from today's birthing experience!

That day, Wilma Jane Baxter was born, whom we would come to call Janie. For Jake and me, it was a moment of pure joy. We had always planned on becoming parents and now, gazing down at our new baby, we felt a kind of fullness that we had never felt before.

Dr. Guernon, on the other hand, was as cold as ever. He helped me deliver the baby, and then promptly made himself scarce, leaving the nurses with no instructions for my care. I spent the next ten days in the hospital (which would be unheard of now, unless there were complications with the birth). I ate all my meals in bed, learned how to breastfeed, and spent plenty of time doting over my new daughter.

At the end of my stay, Dr. Guernon came in to check on me. He walked to my bedside and asked me to get up. Since I hadn't left my bed during those ten days, I got to my feet with quite a bit of difficulty. "Haven't you been walking?" he demanded. "No," I said. "The nurses never told me to do that."

As it turns out, Dr. Guernon had not instructed the nurses to encourage me to get up on my feet and walk around, so they didn't. And I, as a new mother, didn't even think to ask. As a result, I was stiff, sore, and quite irritated with Dr. Guernon. But before I could express my annoyance, he plucked baby Janie from my arms and slammed her down on the exam table! The doctor must have seen me wince because he turned and said to me, "She's a baby. You don't have to treat her like glass."

Looking back, I might have said something to Dr. Guernon, but, as I mentioned, I was a first-time mother with little preparation. We didn't have all the books on parenting that exist today. We simply did our best, consulted other parents, and trusted our instincts.

LIFE IN THE DUPLEX

It wasn't long after Janie's birth (and the end of World War II) that we were asked to leave our apartment on Hill Street. "Newborns use too much water," the landlord claimed. "You can't have a baby here."

Although it was completely unfair, we didn't protest. We were back to square one, combing the city for an apartment that fit both our needs and our slim budget. Fortunately, Janie was a great baby and tolerated all the commotion with a cheerful little smile. I was even able to bring her out to friends' homes when we were playing bridge. She would either sleep or quietly watch whatever was going on with her big, round eyes. She was such a good baby, it was no wonder we wanted to have another one!

Eventually, with the help of Mr. Chumley, we found a duplex on Locust Street, right on campus. Part of me loved living right in the thick of things—I had, after all, grown up with a constant stream of neighborhood kids, church members, and perfect strangers passing through my family's door and sharing our table.

In our duplex, Jake and I would sometimes host friends of ours for card games. At the time, we were friends with our minister, Henry Cox, and his wife, Eleanor, and would often invite them over on Sunday nights. One memorable night, we were playing canasta, and Jake and Henry were on a hot streak. Between the two of them, they had all of the highly coveted red threes, twice in a row. On the third hand, they declared that, once again, they had the red threes.

I said, "Again? I don't believe you."

"We do," Henry insisted. "Want to bet?"

Being my stubborn self, I said, "Sure. I bet that you don't have those threes."

"Okay," Jake said. "If you're wrong, you'll have to push a peanut across the carpet with your nose."

It was a ridiculous wager, but I agreed, knowing that we didn't have any peanuts in the house. When the fellows laid down their cards to reveal the four red threes, I was astounded!

"Well, you win," I said, "but I can't follow through with the bet because we don't have a single peanut in the house."

"Oh yes we do!" Jake pointed to a spot on the rug. There, half-hidden in the shag carpet, was a solitary peanut.

After our laughter died down, I declared, "There's no way I'm pushing a peanut across the carpet with my nose."

"But you have to honor the bet," Henry insisted. "Well," he said, a smile creeping across his face, "how about we change the terms? Instead of pushing the peanut, you have to bake us a cherry pie every Sunday for four weeks. How does that sound?"

"Deal!" I said. At the time, we had a prolific cherry tree and I was already making pies like they were going out of style—so many, in fact, that our freezer was filled to the brim with them. It was a good thing we had purchased our freezer—an appliance we had acquired by diligently saving S&H Green Stamps. We traded in fifty-five books of stamps for that freezer!

Because of my enthusiasm for pie-baking, my nose and my pride were saved that evening...and we all enjoyed plenty of pie that month!

In addition to canasta, we learned how to play bridge from our dear friends, Leo and Genevieve Cox. Jake met Leo through his work at Chanute Field, and they quickly became friends. Before we knew it, the four of us were playing regular games of bridge either at our home or theirs, with baby Janie in tow. Little did I know, this hobby would become one of my favorite pastimes and a great way to connect with people later in life.

Jake and I became enthusiastic bridge players and, in addition to playing bridge with the Cox's, we joined another couple's bridge group. If that wasn't enough, I also joined a *third* bridge club in town at the invitation of a church friend. The club was founded by four young women when their husbands had been away in the service. They played for a few years before deciding they wanted to expand and include a second table. So, each of the four women invited a friend...and I happened to be one of the friends. It was a diverse group of people (all denominations, as we used to say), made up of people from the University, our church, and other members of the community nearby. What started as a casual invitation, turned into over three decades of bridge-playing!

Years later, after Oscar Plumb became our minister, Jake and I became part of yet *another* social group. We were comprised of seven couples from church, and we called ourselves the Fun Club. There were Dorothy and Bob Atkins, Tom and Odele Whetzel, Helen and Glen Stout, Paul and Harriette Clinebell, Bob and Mary Wright, and Oscar and Helen Plumb. We would get together on weekends, have a potluck dinner, play cards, and talk late into the night. Even though our home wasn't terribly large, when the group came to our house we made due by rolling out a ping pong table (handmade by Jake) and covering it with a tablecloth I had made using a sheet. That makeshift table was used for both our potluck dishes and as a place to play our table games.

Our Fun Club friendships extended beyond cards. We often traveled together, going all over the U.S. with our caravan of cars and camping gear. To this day, I still keep in touch with some of the Fun Club members.

* * *

The duplex on campus quickly felt like home. Jake and I loved to keep busy, and our home was conveniently positioned near the action. We attended football games, basketball games, church events, band competitions, and many other activities on or near campus. The one disadvantage, however, was that we lived close to First Avenue—a busy, four-lane street that passed by a couple of fraternity houses, a bustling apartment complex, and a few other residences. Cars would stream down this street, heading toward or away from campus.

As you can imagine, we had to be cautious in this area with gregarious young Janie. That's why when Janie, at the age of three, left her playmate and took a walk alone, I was beside myself with fear! Pregnant at the time, I headed toward First Avenue to look for her. My imagination ran wild, picturing Janie hit by a car or taken in by some stranger.

When I was partway down the street, I glanced at one of the fraternity houses, and there was Janie! She sat on the front porch, talking with animated hands to a group of fraternity boys. They smiled and laughed, listening to the tales spun by her three-year-old mind.

"Janie!" I called. "You get over here this minute!"

But Janie shook her head and refused to leave the fraternity house porch. She was having such a good time, she didn't want to go.

I walked to the porch, grabbed her by the hand, and started leading her away. "I'm going to have to give you a spanking," I said, "so that you remember to never, ever do that again."

Janie was crying by this time, sad that I had pulled her away from the fun *and* anxious about her first spanking. When we reached the front steps of the duplex, she squatted down and cried, "Please don't spank me! Please don't spank me!"

Even though it was difficult for me, I knew that if I said I would do something, it was important for me to follow through. I bent Janie over my knee and gave her a few light swats on the behind. She cried, but I'm certain Janie's first spanking hurt *me* more than it hurt her.

Of course, when Jake came home that night, Janie ran to him right away, crawled onto his lap, and told him about the spanking. Jake hugged her and bounced her on his knee, soothing her crying. That was the way things would go as Janie and her sister-to-be grew up. I would discipline them for something and then they would run to Jake, who would shower them with affection and rock away their troubles on his knee. I swear the girls thought he was a saint!

But that was Jake—level-headed, rarely upset. In fact, I only ever *really* saw him mad on two occasions. The first time occurred when we were young and still living in Montgomery, and he wanted to give me his picture. He had left it in his room and, before he could give it to me, a guy named Whalen found the picture, took it, and gave it to me. To this day, I'm still not sure why Whalen did that, but boy, was Jake mad! I thought he was ready to wind up and give Whalen a punch in the jaw, but he didn't. I don't think Whalen forgot about the incident anytime soon, though.

The other time I saw him get really, truly mad was when he was a chairman of the building committee of our church in Champaign. The church wanted to refurbish the sanctuary and was working with an architect on the plans. Well, Oscar, the preacher, kept changing his mind about the sanctuary plans and, each time he wanted an addition here, a modification there, the architect had to redo the plans, and *that* cost money. Practical Jake grew increasingly irritated every time Oscar changed his mind. Finally, he reached the end of his rope when Oscar wanted to add a set of stairs leading up to the altar. They argued, and the whole thing ended with Jake in a rage. I don't think there are many people who can say they've only displayed anger twice in front of their family…and half of those angry moments were caused by a preacher! By the way, the remodel *did* include those steps to the altar, despite Jake's irritation.

CHALLENGES IN CHAMPAIGN

I am forever grateful for the years Jake and I had together. He was a wonderful father and did a great job helping to raise the girls. We had originally wanted to have six children, but God had different plans for us. Two years after Janie was born, I miscarried.

Any woman who has held a child in her womb, only to have it swept away in a moment, knows how devastating that experience is. I mourned the loss of my child, but understood that it was all part of a divine plan. I picked myself up and kept going.

Jake and I had season tickets for the University's football game and we thought it might be good for my spirits to go to a game. We called the doctor, and he gave permission for me to attend, as long as I didn't get overly excited. So, just one day after I miscarried, we went to a game. I think it was Jake's way of distracting me from the deep loss I had just experienced. He was always one to offer unconditional love and support. I'd like to think that I was there for Jake, too, when he needed me.

When Janie was about three years old, and I was pregnant once more, Jake suddenly lost his Civil Service job. It was a difficult blow, as he loved his work and the community he had found in his department. He was not fired for misconduct or budget cuts or any of the usual reasons for sudden unemployment. Instead, he was pushed out of his position because the service men had all returned from the war and were in need of employment. Though he didn't want to leave his job, he did what he had to do and stepped aside so a war veteran could take his place.

We had no savings and couldn't get by off my scant earnings as a secretarial substitute, so Jake set out looking for new work. Luckily, he had many talents and a sterling reputation as a hard worker, so it wasn't long before he was able to land another job. A friend at our church connected Jake with an opportunity at the Champaign Builder's Supply Company, where Jake became the office manager. It turned out to be an excellent position, as he was able to purchase building supplies at cost, which we would later use to build our home on Garfield Street.

We breathed a sigh of relief and carried on. And, once again, I thanked God for watching over us.

The church had always been a pillar in the center of our lives and now, during these challenging times, we needed it more than ever. One of the first things we had done when we moved to Champaign was find a church, and it was through that church—the Champaign First United Methodist Church—that we made close friends, taught Sunday School and vacation Bible school, mentored youths, and went on the occasional church retreat, work camp, or camping trip. It's hard to express the enormity of the church's impact on our lives. I am forever grateful for our church community and all the help and support we received over the years from those kind people.

KATHY ARRIVES

Jake and I worked through the challenges of miscarriage and unemployment together, and we were finally able to focus on the excitement of having our second child. My third pregnancy was a difficult one. I was often sick, but I made it to full term...only to find out that the baby was breech and couldn't turn around on her own. Our doctor—Doctor Moss, Jr.—decided that the baby had to be delivered by caesarean section. It wasn't terribly common at the time, but it was getting to be less dangerous than it had been in the past. With the due date close, Dr. Moss asked me, "When do you want to have this baby? We could deliver it as soon as tomorrow."

My eyes grew big as saucers; I had not been prepared for a delivery so soon. "Tomorrow?" I said. "Could we do the next day? I have a baby shower tomorrow, and I think I should be there."

I'm probably one of the only women in history who wanted to carry a full-term baby *longer* than I had to, but I was determined to have my baby shower!

April 29th, 1949 arrived and, after a smooth procedure, I had a second beautiful little girl in my arms. Kathy Ann Baxter was given her name by little Janie, who had a friend named Kathy Lynn. We liked Janie's suggestion and agreed that it was a pretty name for a little girl.

After Kathy's birth, I had to recover in the hospital for ten days. I remember my stitches hurting and having difficulty with bending. The doctor had me wear a device called a "mini tail binder" to help support my newly stitched abdomen. I happened to be in the hospital at the same time as a friend of mine, and she remarked at how straight I was standing.

"Yeah, I suppose," I replied. "Just don't ask me to bend for anything!"

When I took Kathy home, Jake and I were filled with joy. She was a good little baby, and quite the character! Those early days were an indicator of the little social butterfly she would eventually become. Her precious smiles and giggles tugged on our heartstrings, and soon we could not imagine our lives without her. Janie was a caring older sister and the girls eventually became close friends—a friendship which continues to this very day.

THE HOUSE ON GARFIELD STREET

With Jake's new job at the Builder's Supply Company, we decided it was time to give ourselves a little more space and build a home of our very own. At the edge of town, we found a string of three empty lots for sale and purchased one of them for our dream home. Over the course of a year, Jake consulted with a friend who specialized in building pre-manufactured home foundations. Little by little, Jake purchased supplies at-cost and built the foundation for our new house from the ground, up.

When the pre-cut house was placed on the foundation and it was finally complete, you could *not* imagine my excitement. This wasn't just a place to settle into temporarily; this was a place to grow roots and make our own.

Jake planted a big garden (putting down literal roots), in which we grew all kinds of vegetables that I used for canning. In addition to fresh vegetables, we also received fresh meat every spring, after Jake's parents butchered and smoked their hogs. The girls liked the fresh ham so much that when I asked Janie what she wanted her dad to plant in the garden, she replied, "Ham, just like Grandpa Baxter sends us!"

I also made homemade tomato juice, which the girls refused to drink unless it was served in our nice Fostoria glasses! My mentality is this: why keep your nicest possessions locked away your entire life? You might as well take them out and enjoy them. You can't take them with you when you're gone. Because of this belief, the girls got their wish and were able to use the Fostoria glasses.

Jake and I always cared more about *people* than *things*. We were quick to host events at our new home and, just like our little duplex, the house on Garfield bustled with activity. Not only did we continue to hold the occasional game night with Fun Club, we also opened our home to the youth we mentored in our church, foreign exchange students at the University, cadets at Chanute Field, and neighbors. Anyone who needed a good meal, a little conversation, or a place to celebrate the holidays was welcomed into our home.

When the girls were young, Jake and I started mentoring a group of college-aged students from our church through the Methodist Youth Fellowship program. I remember a couple of the guys would stop by our home and talk with Jake for hours, long into the night. At the time, I was a little peeved (especially because we had two young children and sleep was a precious commodity!), but three of these men went on to become ministers, so my lack of sleep was a small price to pay.

Living close to campus, we were surrounded by ambitious young people from many different walks of life. For me, their energy was contagious. Jake and I loved immersing ourselves in the action—going to sporting events, watching band rehearsals and competitions, or simply making friends with the students and welcoming them into our home. Some of these students ended up being good friends and would drop by and see us regularly.

A student named Terry was a particular favorite of Janie and Kathy. His smile could light up the room, and he loved to tell animated stories, complete with different voices and hand gestures. The girls enjoyed Terry so much that they started requesting him as a babysitter (we used a sitter every Sunday night when we attended church with our college group *and* every Wednesday night, when we had choir rehearsal). Soon, Kathy refused to even consider another sitter. She'd say, "No. I 'ist' want Terry, 'ist' Terry." Sometimes, we would even make special trips to the college campus to watch the band practice, because Terry was one of the clarinet players.

I truly believe the constant stream of students in our home was good for the girls. They learned—just as I did as a child—how to be around and get along with a wide variety of people from all different backgrounds. These students opened up their little worlds and gave them a glimpse into the diverse lives and backgrounds of others. I remember how fascinated they were when we hosted two students from Korea. These young men were studying at the University and didn't have anywhere to go during the holidays. So, naturally, we invited them into our home and, in return, they told us all about their home country and occasionally brought gifts.

Even though these students hailed from the same country, they were very different and came from different social backgrounds—one of the young men was part of an upper-class family, while the other was less well-off. This was another important lesson for the girls (and for me), as it taught us the importance of getting to know individuals, rather than making snap judgments about them, based on their culture.

We regularly hosted those students for two years and kept in touch for several years after that. The upper-class student gave me a lovely, mother-of-pearl inlaid vase, and I still keep it displayed on my shelf. On another occasion, two cadets from Chanute Field came for Thanksgiving Dinner. We invited them back for Christmas, and they brought the girls a pair of gigantic stuffed animals, shaped like frogs, which were an instant hit.

TYPING INTO THE NIGHT...

Many of my best memories tie back to the house on Garfield Street and our early years in Champaign. The magic that comes from having a house of your own is difficult to describe. In those early years on Garfield Street, I spent almost all of my time inside that house—tending to the girls, keeping house, and working from the little office that Jake set up for me upstairs.

My office was my haven. I had my own desk, a typewriter, and plenty of carbon paper. There was no air conditioning at the time, so I would open the dormer windows on either end of the loft and let the air flow through the space as I worked.

I began taking typing assignments from University students and professors. They would give me hand-written dissertations or professional research, and I would type them up. Since I had wanted to stay at home with the girls, this occupation was perfect for me. I enjoyed learning about all kinds of diverse topics as I click-clacked away on my Underwood typewriter. I like to say, if I could remember everything I ever typed, I'd be the smartest woman in the world!

Our neighbor girl, Margene Kirkwood, occasionally helped me with proofreading the papers. Years later, she would tell me, "I used to hear you clacking away on your typewriter half the night!"

It's not much of an exaggeration. I kept busy with my work, charging $.20 per page, and $.01 per carbon copy. It was a low fee, considering some of the terrible handwriting I had to interpret! One of my toughest projects was a paper written in Old English. The student used the Old English alphabet, complete with its strange symbols and spellings. I had to bring his half-completed paper to his house one time to ask about a few difficult-to-interpret phrases. He wasn't at home, so I asked his wife about the phrases.

"Beats me!" she said. "I think *he* can hardly interpret this stuff." She shot me a grin and added, "I'm glad you are typing this because we probably would have ended in divorce!"

Most of my work was more straight-forward. I would type up term papers, dissertations, or even books that were written out in long-hand. I was a fast worker and could type like greased lightning. The word got out that I was an excellent typist with reasonable fees, and I was rarely without some kind of project.

One couple from our church—Ben and Jen—caught wind of my work and asked if I could type a few marketing materials for their company. I accepted, knowing that Ben and Jen were distributers for Tupperware, a company that was quickly gaining traction. I typed up flyers for Tupperware parties, monthly newsletters, and other internal communications. I also cut stencils, which could be used for making copies in a mimeograph machine. When I first started typing research papers and essays, I had no idea I would someday do work for such high-profile customers.

WE ARE FAMILY

Though Jake and I worked hard, we always made time for family. The girls were an endless source of entertainment and we enjoyed watching them develop their distinct personalities. Janie was pleasant and sharp as a whip, but could also be serious and sensitive. Her first grade teacher, Miss Rose, once reported that it was impossible to discipline other students without poor Janie bursting into tears!

Kathy was creative, smart, and a social butterfly. When the girls were in elementary school, they would walk home every day for their lunch. It was a short walk—four blocks or so—but somehow Kathy always managed to be late. She was too busy visiting with friends to come home when she was supposed to. One day, I decided that this nonsense had to end and said, "Kathy, I've told you time and again that you need to come straight home for lunch. I'm going to have to discipline you somehow. This afternoon, I want you to think about what you would do if you had a little girl that did this, and tell me what you come up with after school."

Kathy gave me a serious nod, and I could tell her little wheels were turning. I sent her off to school and I watched her flit away, wondering what she would come up with.

As soon as I saw Kathy after school, I knew she'd been thinking about what I'd said. Her mouth was grim, forehead scrunched in a serious expression.

"Well," I prompted, "did you think about what I said?"

"Yes," she answered. "I 'ist' decided that if I had a little girl that did that…well…I'd give her one more chance."

I couldn't help the laugh that escaped my lips. I tried to keep a straight face as I said, "Kathy, I think that's a good idea. You're going to get one more chance, and no more." She was never late for lunch again.

Both the girls added so much levity and brightness to our lives—constantly making us laugh with their little sayings, antics, and bits of childish wisdom. They were different in some ways, with different personalities and habits, but they also had a lot in common. They both loved music; they both enjoyed camping and hiking in the great outdoors; and they both decided to pursue teaching careers after high school. If they didn't get along as well as they did, our family outings and annual vacations would have been miserable! But the girls were great— cramming into our station wagon or into the family tent without complaint.

Every summer, Jake and I would take a two-week vacation and visit our families in West Virginia—one week with the Dents, and one week with the Baxter's. The girls were good sports most of the time, but we did have a few struggles (as any normal family on vacation would). While staying in the Baxter family's rustic house on the creek, I started to notice that Janie wasn't saying grace at the dinner table. I pulled her aside and asked, "What's the matter with you? Why aren't you saying grace? You always say it at Grandmother Dent's house."

Janie crossed her arms and gave me a serious look. "Grandma and Grandpa Baxter have an outdoor bathroom and I'm sure not grateful for that!"

I had to laugh because *I* also wasn't grateful for the Baxter's lack of indoor plumbing! They didn't end up putting in indoor plumbing until the mid-1950s, a year after they were able to get electricity that far up Proctor Creek Road. Jake and Wilma's husband, Earl Van Camp, wired their house for electricity, and Jake's parents were forever grateful to their son and son-in-law.

It wasn't long after the "grace incident" that Jake and I decided that two weeks was a lot of grandparent time for the girls. We started cutting our visits to West Virginia down to one week, and would use the other week to explore different parts of the country. Armed with a tent, some sleeping bags, and little else, we would camp in the wilderness of Minnesota, Indiana, Michigan, West Virginia, Ohio…anywhere we decided to go.

Clever Jake built a fold-down camp kitchen that could be utilized as a food prep area or table. He also made a car-top storage locker to house our tent and larger objects. One time, we were ready to take off on a trip when I noticed that the storage locker was open slightly. I went to close it up and heard a faint whimpering coming from inside.

"Girls!" I shouted. "What's this?"

They exchanged guilty looks and said, "That's Suzy."

Suzy was our miniature Manchester Toy Terrier. She was a good little dog—loving and loyal—and the girls adored her...obviously!

"Girls," I said, "until Suzy learns how to cook, we have to leave her behind."

Suzy-the-dog stayed behind.

I enjoyed each and every one of our vacations, even our memorable "pretend vacation!" During the summer of 1967, we were all set to return to New Haven, Connecticut to visit our old stomping grounds by Yale University. Jake's sister, Wilma, was going to accompany us and she had already traveled from Ohio to Champaign so that we could all carpool together. The day before we were scheduled to leave, Jake's boss called and said he was sick. The boss apologized for the inconvenience, but the company was so small that no one else besides Jake was able to fill in.

Just like that, our trip was canceled. All our excitement drained like air rushing out of a popped balloon. For a few minutes, we were upset about the sudden change of plans. Then, we decided to make the best of a rotten situation. We would have our very own "pretend vacation," or, what people today might call a "staycation."

During the next week, we relaxed and enjoyed each other's company both at home and around town. We each chose a day of the week and planned special activities and meals for that day. Kathy took us mini golfing; Jake decided to take us to a nearby dinner theater; Janie staged a car wash and we splashed around and washed our vehicles. I wanted a set of China dishes—something I'd been dreaming about for a long time—so I decided to take us all on a shopping trip to Robeson's

Department Store. Wilma's chosen activity was to watch home movies and slides. For her meal, she prepared her famous chicken and noodles with apple pie for dessert. I have fond memories of those noodles!

Even though we all would have loved to visit New Haven, our pretend vacation was just as fun and relaxing. It also reinforced what we already knew—that being around each other was more than enough.

SCOUTS

Jake and I were always volunteering for one thing or another. We helped with the church's youth group, taught Sunday school, and chaperoned the girls' band trips when they were in high school. I was active in the United Methodist Women's group, while Jake was active in the Methodist Men's group. In addition to all that, we did a host of other volunteer activities.

One of my fondest memories of being a band chaperone was a weekend trip Kathy's band took to Chattanooga, Tennessee. I have always found historical sites to be fascinating and, during this trip, we were able to visit the Civil War Museum and a couple other historical sites. My love of historical sites was apparent on our family trips too. We visited places like President Lincoln's childhood home and Mt. Vernon (George Washington's family home). I'll always remember how Janie and Kathy thought the best part about Mt. Vernon was rolling down the nearby hill!

As a volunteer, I had plenty of other adventures as the Troop Leader of Girls Scout Troop 64. I started as an assistant to the Brownie Troop Leader when Janie was in second grade and enjoyed all our little activities—knot-tying, camping, arts and crafts. When the Troop Leader decided to step down the next year, I volunteered to take over. Little did I know, I would lead that group of about twenty girls all the way through high school.

In addition to the Scouts' annual summer camping trips (I was one of the few mothers who actually enjoyed the trips!), I led the girls in volunteer excursions, survival skill-learning (such as starting campfires), and a number of other fun activities. We often sang together and would always go caroling at Christmas.

When Kathy was young, she was so upset that she couldn't join the older scouts in their caroling that it brought her to tears. I couldn't bear seeing her like that, so I came up with a solution: Why not gather some of the neighborhood kids and go caroling around the area?

That was the start of a tradition that lasted through the girls' high school days. We would gather fifteen to twenty neighborhood kids, go door-to-door in the neighborhood, and sing our hearts out. It was always a treat for me to hear those young voices harmonizing Christmas carols and laughing as we walked from house to house. At the end of the caroling, I would serve cocoa and cookies and revel in the camaraderie of the kids. I always did love having a full house, teeming with laughter, singing, and story-swapping.

Most of the time, I enjoyed chaperoning the kids, and when I took over as leader of Troop 64, I thought it would be right up my alley. I was right…most of the time. I loved laughing and learning alongside the girls, but there were times when it was a challenging role, especially if the Fearsome Foursome was involved! This was the name I gave to a group of four girls who loved to cause mischief. They were fine individually, but when they got together, they could be holy terrors.

They would pull pranks and play all kinds of jokes on the other scouts. Once, when we were on an overnight camping trip, the Fearsome Foursome covered the outhouse hole with Saran wrap! They pulled this little stunt at night, of course, when no one could see the opening.

Another time, one of the scouts approached me, wringing her hands, nervous as heck, and said, "Those girls are planning something—I don't know what, but it has to do with straws."

I smiled knowingly and said, "I think I know what they have in mind. If you hear something in the middle of the night that sounds like gun shots, ignore it. They're mashing two straws together, and when you pull them apart, they make a loud crack."

Once the scouts wised up to what the girls were up to, the straw prank fell flat. The next morning, one of the Fearsome Foursome approached me and asked, "How did you know what we were up to?"

I told her, "Honey, you can't think of *anything* to do that I haven't already done."

Aside from the Fearsome Foursome pranks, our camping trips were fun-filled and relaxing. We hiked, swam, went canoeing, and enjoyed a campfire—and campfire songs—every night. We'd often stay in Shakamak Park, where there was an area designated for scout troops. Although we were not in close proximity to other troops, we'd occasionally bump into them—especially once the girls got older and the Boy Scouts found us around the camp!

I was always looking for the next adventure and was game to try just about anything with the troops. That's just my personality—jumping into things with both feet. At one point, I decided to apply for a future troop trip to Mexico that would take place the summer after their junior year of high school. The Girl Scout organization had cabañas in Cuerna Vaca where troops could stay and go on daily excursions in the area. Unfortunately, when I applied I was told that there was a four-year waiting list to stay in the cabañas. But do you think that deterred me? Of course not! I decided that we would simply stay in a hotel in the area and do some of the same activities and trips that the other scouts did.

At the time, I didn't realize what an incredible risk I was taking. Here I was, in charge of twenty girls in a foreign country, speaking no Spanish and blindly hoping that everything would go according to plan. By the grace of God—and with a little luck—everything *did* go according to plan and we had an amazing (transformative, really) time in Mexico.

We explored all over the country, including Mexico City, Taxco, and Acapulco. We toured the Glass Factory, walked through a giant shoe workshop, explored the silver mines in Taxco, and climbed the Aztec pyramids on the outskirts of Mexico City. We also visited the Girl Scout cabañas in Cuerna Vaca for a day, and when the girls found out that the troops staying there had to do daily chores, they decided they had lucked out!

Wherever we went, we stood out like a sore thumb—not surprising with a group of twenty young Caucasian women. The girls enjoyed the attention, especially when we went to dance clubs. They would take over the dance floor and do the "twist," which was popular in the U.S. at the time. These dance nights inspired one of the girls to later write an article for the Champaign New Gazette paper with the title, "Girl Scouts Twist Their Way Through Mexico." We never stayed out *too* late at those clubs, especially after one experience when the female emcee, wearing a long dress with thin black straps, dropped one shoulder of her dress and said, "And now for the more intimate part of our program." Our driver quickly jumped to his feet and said, "I think it's time for the scouts to leave." You'd better believe we scooted right out of there! For the rest of the trip, the girls had fun imitating the woman by dropping one shoulder and copying her little phrase in the same husky voice.

The trip was a transformative experience for both the girls and me—stepping outside our culture, meeting new people, exploring new foods (I particularly remember the blazing hot chili), and witnessing how others lived their daily lives. I even picked up a new skill while I was there…

In Acapulco, we had a chance to try waterskiing in the ocean. The tour company guaranteed that each of us would learn within ten minutes, or there would be no charge. As always, I was up for the challenge. I had tried waterskiing in the past, but had yet to do it successfully. This time, however, the instructor was in the water with me and showed me how to sit back, resist the pull of the rope, and let the boat guide me to my feet.

I finally did it! That day in Acapulco, with the sun beating down and the girls cheering me on, I began a lifelong love of waterskiing.

In fact, I continued to waterski until age sixty-eight (the last time took place at Table Rock Lake in Missouri). My whole life, the word "sure" has been my downfall! That's how I found myself up in a hot air balloon in my eighties and white water rafting at age ninety-one. Although I might not have done those activities without a little encouragement from others, I'm happy I did them. They have all been experiences that have added texture and depth to my life.

When I took those scouts to Mexico, some thought I was crazy (and maybe I was, a little), but I considered it to be just another one of life's mini adventures. On our final day in Mexico, I rounded up all twenty girls and we made our way to the train station. The girls piled into the train, and I handed over our tickets to the conductor. He took one look at them and said, "These are not valid. You're going to have to buy new ones."

My heart nearly froze in my chest. "What do you mean?" I asked. "The last conductor took our roundtrip tickets and gave us these receipts for our return trip."

"He shouldn't have done that," the conductor said, shaking his head. "If what you're saying is true, he took your return tickets and gave you worthless receipts for them. He'll probably sell the actual tickets to make a little money on the side. But, there's nothing I can do. You have to pay for new tickets."

My stubbornness kicked in and I stood my ground, refusing to pay for new tickets. We argued for a little while and, in the end, the conductor relented and allowed us to take the train back to Illinois.

When we pulled up to the station in Champaign and I spotted Jake waiting on the platform with Kathy, I burst into tears. Only then did it strike me how lucky we all were to have made it back, safe and sound. My life has been filled with this kind of good fortune, and I'm certain I've had a lot of help from above.

LIFE GOES ON IN CHAMPAIGN

Life in Champaign took a turn after my father died. I was not even forty years old yet—young to lose a parent—and his death was hard to bear. At the time, my parents had been living with Adrah and her husband, Don, in Indiana while Don finished his Ph.D. Shortly after my father's passing, Adrah and Don decided to move to the countryside in New Jersey and start a life there.

My mother felt anchorless. She was still reeling from losing my daddy, and now she was facing the prospect of moving to rural America—a terrifying thought for a through-and-through city girl.

One night, she was talking to Jake on the phone about her dread of moving to rural New Jersey. "I've always lived in a place with sidewalks," she told him.

"Well," Jake replied, "we have sidewalks here. You can come live with us."

He didn't think twice before offering my mother a place to stay. He simply knew it was the right thing to do. That was Jake. Big-hearted and generous.

Just as my daddy and mother had welcomed Grandma Dent into their home when I was a child, so too did Jake and I open our home to my mother. She moved in with us shortly after Jake had offered her "a place with sidewalks," and became my housemate for twenty-three years. For the most part, I was happy to have her company and valued her as a friend and confidant. She was always helpful around the house, loved to sing, and was great at keeping herself entertained. She had a thirst for knowledge and a curious mind, so she would teach herself how to do new things, such as learning how to use a typewriter. At the time, I was working as the church secretary at Champaign United Methodist, so my typewriter wasn't in use as much as it had been in the past. Mother was free to type away!

I loved my position as church secretary, even though it came with a modest salary and no benefits. Before I was hired, I discussed my new role with the minister, saying, "I won't need any coffee breaks, just Kathy breaks!" Fortunately, the job was flexible and, of course, I was working with people whom I already knew well and enjoyed being around. I ended up working as church secretary for six years.

During this time, I continued volunteering at the church, specifically with the United Methodist Women (UMW). I held every officer position over the years, except for treasurer. Believe me, you don't want me in charge of tracking finances!

Growing up in Montgomery, my sisters, mother, and I were charter members of WSCS (Women's Society of Christian Service), the organization that would later come to be called United Methodist Women. It was a brand new organization at the time, and it was exciting for us to have a special designated group just for women of faith. Over time, the organization has spread to every corner of the U.S., as well as across the globe. Having such a group is so important for developing a sense of community among Methodist women, especially for those who are new to the area—it's a built-in way to make friends.

Though Jake and I were busy with volunteering and work, we would still manage to make time for fun. We loved keeping active and would often take little daytrips with the girls to Lake of the Woods or the ice rink (Jake and I were often the only adults skating alongside our kids), or we would attend the girls' band and choir concerts. Janie played the clarinet for a while, before switching to the baritone saxophone, and Kathy played the clarinet.

Music continued to be hugely important in all our lives, just as it had been when I was growing up. Both girls sang in choir groups at school and church all through high school and college. To this day, they are both still involved in choral groups. It must be in our blood!

During one memorable trip to Grand Tetons National Park, we all sat around the fireplace in the main lodge and sang songs every evening.

We were traveling with a few other couples from our church, and everyone would join in the singalong. A couple people had brought their guitars, and Janie played her autoharp. One night, we sang our first song of the evening and paused to catch our breath. To our surprise, applause rang out from every corner of the lodge. The guests thought we were the night's entertainment! We continued singing, and more and more people began gathering to listen. After a while, the crowd started throwing out requests. "Can you do *My Old Kentucky Home?*" "Can you sing *Home on the Range?*" "How about *Oklahoma?*" "What about *Amazing Grace?*" We complied and ended up singing for a couple of hours!

I'll always remember the pure joy of this trip, surrounded by friends, laughing and singing our hearts out. During the day, we would hike and explore. At night, we would all stay in our travel trailers, which we circled up around a central campfire. It was the summer of 1968 and we were blissfully unaware that this would be our very last trip as a family before Jake passed from our lives.

A CHAPTER CLOSES

Early in 1969, Jake encouraged me to apply for a secretarial position at the University of Illinois. There, I would receive a pension and health benefits—both of which were not offered with my current position as church secretary. The earnings and growth potential were also higher at the University.

I followed Jake's advice and decided to apply for a job as a clerical secretary at the College of Education, at the University of Illinois. It was time for a change and, besides, this opportunity would provide better pay than my freelance typing jobs or my work as the church secretary. With Jake's support, I prepared for my interview and typing test. It was March, 1969, when I was offered the job and accepted my new position. I didn't realize it at the time, but I would end up spending the next eighteen years as a secretary in the College of Education, first doing clerical work and later moving up to the role of Administrative Secretary to the Dean.

The timing of my new employment couldn't have been better—just one more example of God looking out for me. Only seven months later, I would have to rely solely on my own income, benefits, and the modest insurance money I received after Jake's death. We didn't have any savings to speak of—much of our money had gone to help pay for the girls' college tuition, in addition to everyday expenses.

The day came in October, 1969. Janie was in her second year of teaching at Westlake Junior High School in Lombard, Illinois and Kathy was a sophomore in college at Western Illinois University. I remember that Jake had taken the week off to prep the house for painting. The day of his death, I came home for lunch and told him I had something on my mind relating to the movie we had seen the night before with our Sunday school class. I approached Jake to talk about it, but he was getting ready to head out the door to work outside. He kissed me and said, "Hold that thought until tonight. We'll discuss it then."

I returned to work, and Jake continued to work outside. Before leaving that afternoon for his exercise class at the YMCA, he read the day's mail, which included a letter from Kathy. After reading her letter, he turned to my mother and remarked, "Bless her little heart."

At the YMCA, Jake headed to his usual exercise class. Before stepping into the class, he spotted a friend he knew—a physician in town—and stopped to chat. They made a joke about some guy's satin gym shorts, and while they were laughing, Jake slumped to the floor. His friend thought he was warming up to exercise, but soon realized he was in trouble. He rushed to his side and tried to revive him, but it was too late. Jake was gone before he hit the floor.

The autopsy showed that a piece of plaque had moved two centimeters into his heart valve, completely constricting the opening. The heart that had always been so big and generous had stopped beating in an instant.

It's hard to describe the devastation I felt when I found out about Jake's death. It hardly felt real. I called the girls and, together, we tried to process the news. I remember thinking, "I don't think I can do this alone." I didn't want to go on without him; he was such a huge part of my life. We did everything together. We had journeyed through our early college years, found our first real jobs together, built our home, raised our children, acted as constant, loyal companions…and it was all over in the blink of an eye.

Jake had a lovely service. Family, as well as friends from the business community, the college, and the church showed up and packed the church sanctuary. He was well-loved and had many friends. I appreciated all their condolences, but felt overwhelmed at the same time. I had to make so many quick decisions that I wasn't prepared to make—funeral arrangements, burial preferences, financial decisions.

The ten-thousand dollars of life insurance money I received was little consolation. I would have gladly returned it if it meant I could have Jake back in my life. But, here I was, still overcome with grief, and expected to make major financial decisions. My first thought was to pay off the house, but the Vice President of our local bank encouraged me to invest a large portion of the money.

I knew *nothing* about investing and was in no place to teach myself. We had always lived hand-to-mouth, and investing in the stock market seemed like something *other people* did. The VP of the bank sent me to a broker who showed me a few stock options from the Blue Chip Group and asked me to select the companies I wanted to invest in. I did it without much thought, choosing Standard Oil because I saw it had headquarters in New Jersey—my sister lived in New Jersey, so why not? Then, I looked down the list and saw Union Carbide, which had headquarters in Charleston, close to where I grew up. "That one, too," I said, pointing at Union Carbide. "I'll put another $250 into that one."

Well, Standard Oil was purchased by a nice, little oil company known as Exxon, and Union Carbide divided into an entity called Praxair. Unwittingly, my blind investments turned out to be lucky investments.

After all the legal and financial decisions were made, the meals from friends were eaten, and life started to settle down, the real sadness struck. I wasn't sure how I could go forward, and I spent a lot of time praying and asking for guidance. At some point, I decided I wasn't alone. I still had my girls, my mother, my close friends and family, and help from above. And I became convinced that Jake was with me during that difficult time.

One time, I had to fix the chain on a light above the dryer. It had broken right up to the very top, and I was having a dickens of a time getting a hold of that little ball to pull the chain down. I couldn't do it, and I couldn't do it. Finally, I tilted my head up and said out loud, "Jake, if you're up there, will you help me get this fixed?"

Next time I tried, I grabbed a hold of the little nub of chain without any trouble and got it right down. I had no doubt that Jake was right there with me, helping me out.

It was these small daily reminders—broken light fixtures, house repairs, cooking for only myself and my mother—that caused me the most grief in the years that followed. I remember having to bring my vehicle in for a repair for the first time ever. Jake had always been handy and did all our car repairs on his own, so I had no sense of what it costs to get repairs done at an auto shop. When the mechanic handed me the bill, I was so shocked I immediately burst into tears!

Everything was a complete readjustment—a total recalibration of my life. I knew this unexpected twist in my life's path wasn't going to be easy, but I told myself to be strong. I thought, "I'm not the first one to go through this. If others can do it, I can too."

PART III

Life as a Widow

MAKING PEACE WITH WIDOWHOOD

I won't sugarcoat things. Being a widow was awful. There were some days when my heart was so heavy, I felt like I couldn't get out of bed. But I did. I had to be at work by eight o'clock every morning and I showed up faithfully, rarely missing a day. They were good to me at the University—giving me time off if I needed it and providing excellent benefits—and I wanted to return the favor. Besides, my parents taught me to be a loyal employee, and I took that lesson to heart.

I would put on a brave face and pretend that everything was all right. Inside, I was still mourning the loss of my twenty-six-year companion, but on the surface, I'm sure all my co-workers thought I was getting along just fine.

My widowhood lasted eighteen years. At times, I felt incredibly alone; at other times, I felt the love, compassion, and inclusion from my family members, friends, co-workers, and church community. My mother lived with me during this time, and she did much of the cooking and made the house seem less like a ghost town. She was also helpful around the house, assisting me with chores without me asking. Though Kathy and Janie were independent young ladies by this time, they were wonderful and regularly called or came home to see me. As for my friends—well, they were a mixed bag. It's amazing how people show their true colors after a tragedy. Most were supportive and stuck with me for the long-term, inviting me to their get-togethers even when everyone else was partnered with a significant other. Others—such as the friends we made through Jake's work at Builder's Supply Company—seemed to melt away into the woodwork. It was as if our friendships never existed.

Fortunately, the Fun Club, the Cabin Crew, and the Bridge Club still invited me to their card games and get-togethers. I specifically remember Alice Adams from Bridge Club, and her husband, including me in outings to the dinner theater or basketball games. Bob Wright was the track coach at U of I and his wife, Mary, would take me to track meets. Our friends, the Edwards, also included me in their trips to their cabin during the summer. And then there was the church. The church was a welcome distraction, and a refuge from daily hardships. I enjoyed the company of the people there and kept myself busy with all kinds of church-related activities.

I continued volunteering at the church, including teaching Sunday school for the first grade class. I have many fond memories of this class, including making popcorn while studying the five senses…and making everyone in church hungry by filling the air with the buttery scent of popcorn. I also remember some of the students quite well, including little John Wright who later became a receiver for the Detroit Lions. Johnny was a nice little boy, and I was friends with his grandma, Mary. One Sunday, I was teaching a class about sharing and, to demonstrate the concept, we made no-bake cookies which the kids would take home and share with their family members. This was shortly after Jake had died and my mother had just left to visit one of my siblings, so I was truly alone in the house for the first time. Because of that, I didn't feel the need to take any cookies.

One of the little girls noticed and said, "Aren't you going to take some?"

"I don't really have anyone to share them with," I said, doing my best to keep the tears out of my eyes.

That's when little Johnny Wright spoke up and said, "But you have a lot of friends!"

That made me smile, and I realized he was absolutely right. I was lucky to have the kindness and support of so many wonderful people in the United Methodist Church, including his grandparents.

HAWAII

Though being a widow was tough, there were several bright spots during my solo years in Champaign. In 1970, just a year after Jake died, my cousin Esther gave me a call and asked if I would like to join her on a trip to Hawaii. She knew Jake's death had been hard on me and thought a nice vacation would be just what I needed.

She was right, I did need to escape for a little while. Although I had never flown on an airplane before, I thought, "Why not? What do I have to lose?" I agreed to go and began preparing for our trip.

The tour Esther had booked included four Hawaiian islands—Maui, Kauai, Molokai, and the Big Island—and plenty of activities. Since we had to fly between each island, I soon became comfortable with air travel—something I would end up doing *a lot* in later years. We visited a lot of historical sites, as well as a Polynesian cultural center, Japanese gardens, and many other fascinating places. We even attended a couple of traditional luaus with hula dancing and had a chance to eat roasted pork, which we had watched them bury in a fire pit earlier in the day. Our trip was filled with swimming, excellent food, and a few hikes, including one memorable hike to the top of a mountain overlooking the Haleakala volcano. When we reached the summit, our view was unfortunately cloudy and gray. However, on the way back down, the clouds lifted and there was Haleakala, an enormous volcano situated across a rocky plain that resembled the pocked surface of the moon.

All of these excursions were conducted by a tour company, and we followed their schedule pretty closely. However, late one afternoon in Maui we decided to break away from the rest of our tour group, go for a walk along the beach, and have a swim. Esther was a redhead and burned easily during the day, so this was the perfect time to enjoy the ocean, when the shadows were starting to grow long.

As we were walking along the shore, we noticed some commotion in the water. A young boy, maybe seven or eight years old, was flailing around in the waves, his snorkeling mask filling with water. Without hesitating, Esther and I rushed into the ocean. She wasn't as strong of a swimmer as I was, so she anchored herself on a rock as I swam out to grab the boy.

When I reached him, he threw his arms around my neck and pulled himself toward me. I tried to remain calm and focused on keeping a steady stroke as I swam back to the rock where Esther was standing. When I got there, she helped pull the little boy up and take off his mask. He coughed and sputtered, and I knew he would have drowned if we hadn't spotted him and rushed to his aid.

On shore, we sat him down and asked if he had been swimming all by himself. The poor thing was shaken, but he nodded and then pointed to a couple guys down the beach. "My uncle," he managed.

I was incensed. His uncle and the other man were clearly not paying attention, but what could I do?

"Run along," I said and watched him walk back to his family, snorkel in hand. I always wondered what the little boy told his family after that incident. Did he realize how close he'd come to drowning?

After that, Esther and I slowly made our way back to the tour group. We hardly knew how to describe what had just happened, but we agreed that it had been a spiritual moment for us. God had sent us down the beach to rescue that little boy. I think about that boy from time to time and wonder what has become of him.

CATCHING THE TRAVEL BUG

Five years after my trip to Hawaii, I had the chance to fly again. These were sometimes lonely years, and I was still adjusting to the absence of Jake, as well as the girls, who were now young adults with budding careers. I had my mother, but she would leave every summer to visit my siblings, who lived all across the country. Naturally, I tried to fill the empty space and sometimes invited people to dinner, or even rented out a room in the house. In the mid-1970s, I met a Ph.D. student named Seba Ali who was looking for a place to stay. Dean Atkin brought her to me and asked me to help her find a place to live during her six-week stay. No one I contacted wanted to rent to someone for only six weeks, so I told her, "I know of a house that's available. Two old ladies live there, and they would sure like the company."

Of course, I was talking about our house! Seba moved in and we became friends. Six weeks ended up turning into three months, and I thoroughly enjoyed her company. She was originally from India, but had lived off and on in Geneva, Switzerland, where her husband, Liaquat, worked for the United Nations. While she was working on her Ph.D. in educational psychology, she also had to maintain a *very* long-distance relationship with Liaquat, and that was sometimes difficult for her. He visited occasionally, but she tried to go back to Switzerland whenever she could. They had lived there so long, they considered it home.

The summer after she started living with me, she asked if I would be interested in visiting Switzerland. Without hesitation, I said yes (as I often do!) and we started preparing for my two-week trip.

This would be my first trip to a foreign country, aside from the Girl Scout trip to Mexico, and my first international plane ride. Little did I know, I would catch the travel bug and go on many more trips across the globe later in life.

My trip to Switzerland was eye-opening. Never before had I been surrounded by so many worldly and prestigious people. I attended several U.N. functions and got to meet ambassadors, dignitaries, and important politicians. Seba and Liaquat fit in well with this elite crowd, but that wasn't the case outside of their little United Nations bubble. I quickly learned that there's a lot of bias in Switzerland (at least there was when I was there), and people often refused to address Seba or make eye contact with her. Instead, they would talk to me, even though *I* was truly the outsider there.

Seba was always dignified, though, and didn't let the blatant racism bother her. She and Liaquat had worked too hard to let something like a little prejudice get to them. Liaquat was the third son in a rich Indian family, which meant he was entitled to…absolutely nothing. He had to work hard to earn his prestigious U.N. position and every dollar in his pocket. It amazed me that these impeccably-dressed people who drove a Mercedes could be subjected to such horrible bias, just because of the color of their skin.

Another bit of culture shock I had in Europe was seeing nude beaches for the very first time. Seba and I toured around a little, including a trip to France. Since Seba didn't drive, I drove their gorgeous Mercedes all the way to the south of France. The countryside was beautiful, and we made several stops at beaches along the way. To my horror, the beaches were dotted with people who were naked as jaybirds. Being the modest Christian girl that I was, I was mortified by these brazen naked bodies. We were certainly no longer in the Midwest!

Seba was a lovely guide, and we had fun seeing the sites together. That trip to Switzerland and France opened up a new door for me. I started to become excited about the possibility of travel and hoped I would have the chance to go abroad again soon.

THE GIRLS BECOME YOUNG WOMEN

One of the things that sustained me during my widow years were my girls. Janie and Kathy brought true joy to my life, and I was so proud of the young women they had become. Both of them were hard workers and successfully earned their teaching degrees, while also working to make extra income. Both were awarded legislative scholarships, which helped Janie pay for tuition at Northern Illinois University and Kathy pay for Western Illinois University.

Kathy was attending the graduate program at Illinois State when her life was forever changed. She was sharing an apartment with another young lady who was also named Kathy—Kathy Emery. Kathy E. had been friends with a young man named Sam ever since high school, and Sam also happened to be attending Illinois State, working on his Masters of Business Administration degree. Sam and Kathy E. were good friends, so he would come over fairly often to see her and hang out.

One time, he called and my Kathy answered the phone.

"Is Kathy Emery there?" Sam asked.

"Sure, I'll go get her," Kathy replied.

"No, wait," Sam said, "I want to talk to you."

Well, that made Kathy's heart flutter! She had always thought Sam was handsome, but had not wanted to interfere with his friendship with Kathy E.

After that first phone call, Sam started visiting more and more often. When Kathy told me she was seeing Sam, she said, "Mom, when I saw him the first time with Kathy E. I thought, 'WOW.'"

Soon afterwards, my mother and I went to visit Kathy and meet Sam. We brought over steaks for dinner and were preparing them in the kitchen when Kathy pulled me aside.

"So," she said, "what do you think?"

I smiled at her eagerness and said, "Well, I can see why you said 'Wow!'"

Kathy and Sam began to become part of each other's lives, and soon everyone around them was buzzing with talk of the "M" word. Sam's sister was attending the U of I, and she came to stay with me for a short time while she was recuperating from having her wisdom teeth removed. One night, she confided in me and said, "I hope my brother marries Kathy. She makes him laugh…and he doesn't laugh very much!"

Secretly, I hoped they would marry too. Sam and Kathy seemed to fit each other like two puzzle pieces. Besides, I admired Sam's work ethic. He was quite the scholar and not only obtained a CPA and an MBA, but also went on to get a law degree at John Marshall Law School in Chicago. Years later, Sam also proved to be a highly ethical financial manager.

* * *

Sam and Kathy were married on a beautiful June day in 1976, surrounded by family and friends. It was truly a community event. Since both of Sam's parents had died by this time, several of our friends from church offered to throw a groom's dinner for him at our house. As was usually the case with our friends, there was no shortage of food or laughter!

Kathy and Sam chose to have their ceremony at the United Methodist Church in Champaign and were married by Reverend Jack North (who would play a significant role in our lives in the future!). I remember the day clearly.

They filled the church that day with family and friends from all over the country. Kathy looked beautiful in her long, white wedding dress, with Sam smiling at her from the altar. They had three friends play a trumpet trio, and the sound of brass filled the sanctuary. The Jacob R. Baxter Memorial Handbell Choir also played during the ceremony.

Janie was Kathy's maid of honor, and she looked gorgeous in her long green and white flowered dress with a scooped-neck and white ruffles on the front and back. Kathy's three bridesmaids were Karen Anderson (Sam's sister), Jan Clinebell, and Kathy Emery.

I could tell Kathy and Sam loved each other with all their hearts, and I was so excited for them to share a future together. Eventually, that future would include three beautiful children: Samantha Elizabeth, Derek Worstall, and Benjamin Jacob. They are all adults now with children of their own. Samantha and Eric Morales have a little girl named Alexandria Jane. Derek and Stacy have one daughter, Cora Martha, and twin sons,

Samuel Worstall and Wesley Worstall. Ben has one daughter named Freyja Harbor.

A couple years after her marriage, Kathy and I were talking and the subject of grandchildren came up. "I'm not old enough to have grandchildren!" I declared.

Imagine my surprise and delight when two yellow roses were delivered to me at work the next week with a note from Kathy: "Do you think you are old enough yet?" With the arrival of her baby girl, Samantha, in 1980, Kathy decided to devote her time to motherhood and end her six-year run as a teacher (first in Pekin, Illinois and then in Darien). She did, however, work up until almost *the* day Samantha was born.

It's hard to describe the joy of becoming a first-time grandmother. It's nearly like experiencing motherhood all over again, with a new little life to dote over. Except, this time, I was able to experience all of the joy with none of the responsibility!

In March of 2008, Kathy's husband, Sam, died suddenly from a brain aneurysm at the age of fifty-eight. Like me, Kathy had lost the love of her life all too soon.

* * *

Janie, meanwhile, was teaching in Lombard, Illinois. She taught physical education at Westlake Junior High School for five years before she decided it wasn't for her. The kids in that school could be a challenge to work with. As she put it, "I'm supposed to be a teacher, not a disciplinarian."

She also had the uncomfortable task of teaching the kids about the birds and the bees. One time, she was reluctant to address a certain topic and said, "For this...just ask your parents." The next day, one of the students approached her and said, "Well, Miss Baxter, I asked my mom and she said, 'Go ask your dad,' and I asked my dad and he...just smiled."

Clearly, the parents were not going to be helpful in teaching this particular area!

Discontent with her job, Janie knew it was time to throw in the towel, even though she didn't have another job lined up. She had reached the end of her rope and decided she needed a break from teaching.

For that summer, she was unemployed, but she didn't mind too much! She had a nice apartment with a pool and would sometimes babysit three boys for a family that lived in the same complex. One day, she was looking after the boys as they splashed and played in the pool when their father approached her. He was an executive at a large computer company called Control Data.

"How's the job search going?" he asked.

"About like this," she said, gesturing to her lounge chair and the pool.

They laughed and he asked, "So, what kind of job are you looking for?"

"Just one that pays money."

"Well," he said, "would you be interested in working at Control Data? I could get you in for an interview." She applied and started working in the Oakbrook office as a receptionist – a job that seemed like a cake walk after dealing with junior high students.

She was a natural at her work and thrived in the corporate environment. In 1977, she transferred to Minneapolis to work in the Region and Headquarters offices. When people would ask me about Janie's job and what she did, I'd say, "She…works with computers." I didn't know all the particulars of her job, but I knew she was happy.

She retired from Control Data/Ceridian after a successful thirty-five year career and continues to love living in Minnesota.

JACK NORTH

During my widow years, I enjoyed watching my daughters strike out on their own and begin new lives with families and careers. I only wished Jake could have been by my side to meet his first grandchild or to congratulate the girls on their successes. Although I still had my mother as a housemate, life felt empty at times, like there was a piece of me missing.

Despite that feeling, I had no intention of remarrying. It barely crossed my mind, although I eventually softened to the idea of dating other people. Some friends of mine seemed to love playing "matchmaker," and would sometimes set me up on dates. My co-workers were especially keen on connecting me with professors at the University (one professor I dated for a while eventually became the dean).

The pattern, however, was always the same. We would go on a few dates, get to know each other, and when things started to get serious, I would turn and run the other way! I wasn't ready for that kind of commitment, even after years—and then a decade—passed after Jake's death.

I remember dating a man who was a singer in a barber shop quartet. We shared a love of music and seemed to be getting along well…until he asked, "When do we get to the huggy-kissy part?" Again, that was my cue to leave.

It wasn't until the late 1970s that I finally started seeing someone who made me consider the idea of remarriage. That man happened to be the very preacher who presided over both Jake's funeral and Kathy's wedding: Reverend Jack North.

Jack had arrived in Champaign, Illinois in 1967 to start his ministry at the First United Methodist Church. He took over the position of an interim minister, who had been filling in for two years after our beloved minister and dear friend, Oscar Plumb, retired and moved to Florida.

Jack was a driven individual and highly motivated. Before Champaign, he had earned a Bachelor's Degree from Drury University and a Bachelor's of Divinity from Garrett Theological Seminary in Evanston, Illinois. He also received honorary Doctor of Divinity degrees from Illinois Wesleyan University and Wiley College in Texas. Though he and his wife loved their home state of Missouri, Illinois seemed to offer more opportunities for ministers (and the pay and benefits were not nearly as good in Missouri). So, they remained in Illinois, moving whenever the Bishop's Cabinet requested them to do so. He served in churches in Cessna Park, El Paso, Peoria, and Kankakee before moving to Champaign.

Jack and his wife settled into the community, but they were careful to keep a little distance between themselves and the members of the church. Some ministers are cautious about falling into cliques with their parishioners and don't want to be seen as prioritizing some people over others. We all respected the North family's decision and were satisfied with seeing them at occasional church-related celebrations or outings. Though they weren't as close as the Plumbs, we welcomed Jack and his wife, Sarah, into our community. They had four children—Charlotte, David, John, and Becky. Our girls didn't know their children particularly well at the time, but they did participate in a few church activities together.

Today, Jack's family consists of Charlotte, her four children, twelve grandchildren, and twelve great-grandchildren (making us great-great grandparents!); David and Linda, their two boys, and four grandchildren; John and Mary, their three children, and six grandchildren; and Becky, who is a teacher in Guam.

Jack was a well-loved minister and had an amazing speaking voice (though his singing voice left something to be desired!). He spoke in a soothing bass, which never failed to captivate me and others as we listened to his sermons.

After Jack had been at Champaign United Methodist for seven years, his wife, Sarah, died after a decade-long battle with cancer. The year was 1974, and it took him—just as it took me—a few years to recover from his loss and begin dating again. He plunged himself into his work and, two years after Sarah died, he was appointed by Bishop Leroy Hodap to the Cabinet as the District Superintendent of the Pontiac district. As superintendent, Jack kept very busy, which I think was a welcome distraction from the tragedy he had recently experienced. He would travel all over, delivering sermons and checking in with each of the eighty-nine churches in his district.

It was during this time that his now-grown children began encouraging him to get out of the house and start seeing other people. His youngest daughter, Becky, was especially adamant, and she would often help set him up on dates.

One summer in the late 1970s, I was on a date with a professor at a U of I basketball game. He was a smoker and left the stadium at one point to go outside for a cigarette. While I was sitting in the stands by myself, Jack and Becky walked by and spotted me. We talked for a while, and Jack invited me to come sit with them.

I blushed and explained that I was already on a date. Jack was so embarrassed! He apologized and shuffled away, but I remember sitting there and smiling to myself. It was my first inkling that a relationship might be possible between the two of us.

PART IV

A New Chapter

FRIENDSHIP BLOSSOMS

It wasn't long after the basketball encounter that Jack and I began to date. We fell into an easy friendship—I had, after all, known Jack for years and was familiar with his personality and the way he saw the world. Since he no longer lived in Champaign, we maintained a long-distance relationship and would often see each other on the weekends. Sometimes, I would accompany Jack when he traveled to another church to preach (I got used to hearing the same sermons all the time!). Sometimes, he would visit me in Champaign. We both dated other people during this time, but never seriously. I never even held hands with another man, as I didn't want to give the wrong impression.

My new journey with Jack moved at a snail's pace. We took our time and got to know each other well over eight years of dating. Dating later in life is much different than dating during your youth. At this point, our lives were pretty well established. In a way, we had more freedom to take our time and do things our way, without the pressure to define our careers, have children, or build a home. We could simply enjoy each other's company.

We did, however, have to be somewhat discreet with our relationship. Jack didn't want to give the impression that he favored the United Methodist Church in Champaign in any way, so whenever he came to town, the two of us would attend a different church in the city. He became accustomed to introducing me as his "friend," whenever I joined him at one of the churches in his district, a habit that was hard to let go!

The years that we dated were defined by quiet evenings, games with the Fun Club and Cabin Crew, and attending church together. We didn't go out to eat much or do many other activities around town, as we wanted to keep a low profile and not stir up any gossip.

I loved listening to his Sunday sermons in that friendly bass voice. One time, he called the University and asked to speak to me. Another secretary answered and called me over to the phone. "The man on the line has *the* sexiest voice I've ever heard!"

I laughed and took the phone from her. "That's my preacher!" I said.

Jack was patient with me and respected my wish to take things slow. He was also recovering from the loss of his wife and understood very well that the healing process takes time. But it wasn't long before Jack seemed like part of the family. After all, my girls had known him as our minister for many years, and they were comfortable with the idea of the two of us dating. In fact, when Jack was living in Springfield, I stayed with Kathy and Sam when I visited him because they were also living there at the time. I would often spend Saturday night at their home and go to hear Jack preach on Sunday morning.

We became a huge part of each other's lives over those years, sharing everyday joys and humorous moments. Jack was always a jokester and could usually see the humor in a situation. For instance, in the late '70s, Jack was appointed by Bishop Leroy Hodap to be his assistant in Springfield, Illinois. It was a great honor, and Jack gladly accepted. However, when he arrived at his office, he noticed that the sign on his door read:

JACK B. NORTH, ASS. TO THE BISHOP

Struggling not to smile or laugh, Jack walked into Bishop Hodap's office and said, "I'd like you to see something."

Puzzled, Bishop Hodap followed Jack to his office where Jack pointed to the *unfortunate* sign and said gravely, "I believe something needs to be done about that."

Matching Jack's restraint, Bishop Hodap kept a straight face and said, "Yep. Something needs to be done."

Jack served as assistant to the Bishop for six years, first for Bishop Hodap and later for Bishop White. It was Bishop White who would eventually preside over our marriage. I got to know the bishop and his lovely family quite well over the years. Our church was a fairly diverse group, and the fact that Bishop White and his family were African American was never an issue. In fact, he and Jack were able to joke about it. I like to tell the story about the White's welcome dinner that Jack planned. When it was time to enter the dining room, Jack called out, "Now, will the White children please follow me." He paused, realized what he'd said, and everyone in the room burst into laughter. Jack had that effect on people—often light-hearted, he got along well with nearly everyone. He had a kind of charisma that people were attracted too.

Eventually, our lives were so entwined that it made sense for us to take the next step and get married. One evening, after Jack and I had finished washing the twenty-two windows in my house, we sprawled out next to each other on the couch, exhausted. Out of the blue, Jack asked me to marry him.

I was a bit taken aback, but I had known for a while that this would be coming. Smiling, I gladly said yes!

When we called our children to share our news, we got responses like, "It's about time," and, "Finally!" and, "Mother, are you pregnant?"

Shortly after that, Jack asked me to accompany him on a cruise sponsored by Educational Opportunities, a company started by two Methodist ministers who thought it was a good idea for ministers to visit the Holy Land in the Middle East. What started as a small company with occasional trips to Israel, turned into a globally-recognized organization that took clergy of all denominations on trips to religious sites across the world.

Jack had been on many EO trips, but I hadn't yet joined him. The next trip was to the Caribbean and, always up for an adventure, I was eager to go. Jack had booked our accommodations and thought that everything was arranged…until he received a call from EO in his office.

"Jack," the representative said, "we reviewed your application and saw that you wrote in someone named Martha Baxter to join you in your accommodations."

"Yes…" Jack said.

"Well," the EO rep pressed, "It's just that…I'm sorry, but we don't *do* that."

"Okay," Jack responded, ever-cheerful, "I guess I'll just have to marry her then!"

Little did Educational Opportunities know, we had already set our wedding date and would be married by the time we were scheduled to take our trip.

WEDDING BELLS, ONCE MORE

We began to plan for a small wedding. Bishop White, assisted by the current minister, Floyd Stradley, was to marry us in the chapel of the First United Methodist Church in Champaign on November 29, 1985, the day after Thanksgiving. We set this date with our out-of-town family members in mind so that it would be easier for them to attend.

As the date approached, it became apparent that we were going to need more space than just the chapel. All four of my siblings and their families, as well as a good portion of Jake's and Sarah's families, decided to make the journey to Champaign for our wedding. Many of our friends also began to show interest in attending and started asking us about our wedding plans.

At one point, Jack and I just shrugged and said, "Might as well invite the whole congregation!" We announced our wedding in the conference paper and indicated that it was open to the public. Anyone who knew us was free to attend. After that, we shifted our plans and moved the ceremony from the small chapel to the sanctuary.

I've always loved the sanctuary of that church. It has a pleasant, comfortable feeling—like being home. That day, the altar was adorned with a bouquet of bright, multi-colored flowers. I wore a long-sleeved dress that reached just below my knees, purchased from a local dress shop—nothing terribly fancy. Jack and I both appreciated simplicity and our wedding reflected that. We had no professional photographer, no caterer, no professional musicians. What truly mattered was the eternal promise we were making that day, and we tried to keep sight of that.

Though I would have been fine with a small wedding, there was something truly special about looking out over the church—*our* church—and seeing the pews packed with over three-hundred smiling faces of friends and family. Even Jack's Aunt Nettie had made the journey from Springfield, Missouri to Champaign at the age of ninety-nine. At the time, she was the oldest passenger ever to fly on Ozark Air, and the local paper ended up writing a feature about her.

Many Conference ministers were also in attendance, since they knew Jack and wanted to show their support. Later, someone made the comment that it looked like Bishop White had opened up a meeting of the Conference because of all the ministers who had shown up!

What made the day even more special was the participation of our family members in the ceremony and reception. All six of our children stood up with us. My brother, Charles Rea, sang a song based on 1 Corinthians 13, a haunting melody about faith, hope, and love. At the reception in the church parlor, my sister Jane played the piano just as effortlessly and beautifully as ever.

With the assistance of Mary and Linda, we served mints, nuts, and other simple snacks that could easily be replenished if we ran out. We had no idea how many people were going to attend that day, so we had to have a flexible plan. Fortunately, we had enough cake. Our dear friends, the Atkins, bought us a lovely three-tiered wedding cake for the occasion. Even though it turned into a bigger event than we had bargained for, Jack and I felt very blessed that day to have so many wonderful people in our lives.

> Love is patient and kind; love is not jealous or boastful;
> it is not arrogant or rude. Love does not insist on its own way…
> So faith, hope, love abide, these three; but the greatest of these is love
> 1 Corinthians 13: 4,13

TO MISSOURI

After our wedding, Jack and I took a mini honeymoon to Saint Louis, Missouri. It was a snowy, icy journey, but we didn't mind. We were both glowing from the excitement of our wedding and nothing could dampen our spirits.

That Sunday, we attended a service at one of the Methodist churches in Saint Louis. Being well-connected, Jack knew some of the clergy in attendance. After the service, he brought me over to meet them and said, "This is my friend—" he paused and looked at me. "This is my *wife*, Martha."

After years of calling me his friend, Jack could finally introduce me as his wife. The word sounded wonderful to my ears, and it set us both to smiling.

In January of 1986, we went on our first international trip together as a married couple. It was—like many of our trips would be—a cruise through Educational Opportunities. This time, we went to the United Kingdom on the "John Wesley tour." We visited sites that pertained to Wesley, the founder of Methodism, and enjoyed nightly lectures and activities.

After our cruise, we settled back into life as usual, but it soon became apparent to us that things had to change. At the time, Jack was still working as Bishop White's assistant in Springfield, Illinois, which was an hour and a half drive from Champaign, where I was still working at the University. He and I were constantly hopping between the two cities to visit each other, and making the long drive was getting tiring. Finally, we decided it was time for us to make a major change.

I had called Champaign my home for over forty-two years, but I was ready to start a new chapter of my life with Jack. A year after our marriage, I retired, put my house on the market, and prepared to make the move to Springfield Illinois. In the meantime, Jack found a duplex that had enough space for both me and my mother, who would be moving to Springfield with us. Just like Jake, Jack welcomed my mother into his life—and home—with open arms.

However, other parts of the transition were not so smooth. I was given a sharp reminder of how bigoted and judgmental some people can be. After putting my house on the market, a few families came to look at it, including a very nice African American family with a ten-year-old boy. This family agreed to my asking price and secured a FHA loan to meet it, while one of the Caucasian families haggled with me and demanded a discount. Naturally, I went with the African American family. Why wouldn't I?

After that, my neighbor across the street raised a fuss, saying I was decreasing the value of the neighborhood properties, and Jake would "roll over in his grave if he knew what was happening."

"I'd like to think Jake was a Christian," I retorted, "and so am I."

Once I make a decision, I never look back. I finalized the sale of my home on Garfield Street and made the move to Springfield, Illinois in the fall of 1986.

We lived in Springfield for only a short time before Jack retired in July of 1986. He had devoted most of his life to serving the church and decided it was time to do other things he loved—traveling, fishing, dabbling in technology. The day after his retirement, we went on an EO cruise to France and Germany with Bishop White and several other ministers we knew. One evening, Jack was asked to do a blessing before dinner. He stood in front of the group of gathered ministers and asked to say a few personal words. He gave a touching speech, peppered with his usual humor. Toward the end of his "few words," Jack looked across the crowd and said, "I have a special message for Bishop White. Bishop, I'm retired as of today…and if you want anything done, anything at all, do it yourself!" Jack always did know how to get a crowd roaring with laughter.

After the cruise, we returned to Springfield for a short time. Jack knew he wanted to move and wrestled with the decision of where to relocate. Though I loved Illinois, I understood why Jack wanted to move. All his adult life, he had served wherever the Bishop's Cabinet assigned him. He had always lived in church parsonages, and I wanted him to be able to make the decision of where we should retire.

Leaving Champaign was a big wrench for me, but I was willing to move anywhere with Jack and helped him talk through the options as he considered Arizona, North Carolina, Florida, and several others. Eventually, he made up his mind to return to his home state of Missouri. I didn't know much about Missouri, but I knew that if Jack would be happy there, so would I. Our move to Missouri marked the beginning of another chapter of my life that would last twenty-four years.

FROM SPRINGFIELD, ILLINOIS TO SPRINGFIELD, MISSOURI

During Thanksgiving of 1986, while we were still living in Illinois, Jack and I took a trip to Springfield, Missouri. We stayed with Jack's Aunt Nettie and decided to look at houses while we were in the area. We met with a realtor that Friday…and by Saturday we had signed the papers for a new house!

Though it was all very quick, I remember being impressed by Springfield and eager to move there. I was a city girl "from the word go" and loved being in the thick of things. Our new home would be close to a hospital, a grocery store, and a high school. Plus, it was located on a cul-de-sac, which meant we would have a nice little quiet corner without much traffic. Everything seemed to be falling into place…everything except my mother.

When she found out that we were planning on moving to Missouri, she didn't take the news well. She was in her eighties at the time, had just moved to Springfield, Illinois a year and a half earlier, and didn't like the prospect of yet another change.

Reluctantly, she agreed to come with us, and we made the move from Springfield, Illinois to Springfield, Missouri at the edge of winter in 1987. Though Jack and I had shared a home in Illinois, our new home in Missouri felt more permanent. We had a clean slate—we could lay out the house exactly as we wanted, decorate, and fill the rooms with all of our things.

Over the years, I had kept up my spoon collection and my cup and saucer collection, as well as a large collection of Hummels. Hummels are little porcelain figurines, designed and produced in Germany, that depict children in all kinds of poses with different objects, such as umbrellas, baskets, or farm animals. I began collecting Hummels when a bridge-playing friend, Bennie Canaday, offered to exchange a Hummel for a large piece of turquoise (which was very popular at the time) that I had found in the girls' toy box. She was an antique dealer and, when she examined the turquoise and saw how valuable it was, she said, "I'd better give you *two* Hummels for this!"

The house in Springfield, Missouri was Jack's first actual home of his own. As a man of the church, he was always furnished with a parsonage. I had advocated for buying a condo or renting an apartment in Springfield, but Jack insisted on buying a house.

"Okay," I finally agreed, after I saw how much it meant to him. "We can buy a house, but I am NOT going to shovel snow or mow the grass. I did that by myself for eighteen years in Champaign, and I'm sick and tired of it."

Jack agreed but, wouldn't you know, during our very first winter in Missouri, he had to have prostate surgery…just when we were struck by one of the biggest snow storms the area had ever seen. We had fourteen inches of snow, and I only had enough energy to shovel a narrow path out to the mailbox. Everyone has a limit, and I had reached mine! Our friend, Dick Stolp, kindly shoveled the rest.

Jack felt bad that I had to scoop all that snow, but it wasn't his fault. These are the crosses anyone must bear when getting married later in life. Health problems are a certainty, and I knew what I'd signed up for.

When Jack recovered from his surgery, he was eager to dive into retired life and start doing all the activities he loved, including travel. He signed us up for a cruise to the U.K., and we soon realized that it would be difficult to leave my mother in Springfield all by herself. It hadn't quite been a year, and she was still adjusting to her new home and didn't know anyone besides the neighbors. It wasn't fair to mother to leave her alone; and it wasn't fair to us to give up travel and experiencing all the things we wanted to experience in our retirement. We all sat down, discussed the situation, and decided that it was best for mother to live with Adrah and Don in New Jersey.

Mother wasn't terribly happy about the decision, especially since Adrah and Don still didn't exactly live in a city, although they had since moved from their big house in the country to a new home located outside of Hopewell, New Jersey. They had designed this home themselves, focusing on utilizing solar power. There were huge tanks stretching from ceiling to floor, filled with water. The sun would filter through the house, heat the water in the tanks and, miraculously, radiate that heat into the house. They also had a wood burning stove between the living room and dining room, but rarely had to use it.

Mother got along well with Adrah, but she was still reluctant to move. She had already moved twice in the past three years and was worn out from it. In the end, I convinced her to go, even though she did her best to dig in her heels and fight the decision. As we were packing up to make the move, mother gave me a stubborn look and said, "I'm not sure I want to go."

I felt deflated. "Mother," I said, "you have to do this for me."

Despite her protest, she understood deep down that this was for the best and agreed to make the move.

It was during Thanksgiving of 1988 that we moved mother to New Jersey. She lived with Don and Adrah for only a matter of months before she died in the spring of 1989. Up to the end, she was strong, adaptable, and steadfast in her morals. She was and still is a major influence in my life.

LIFE WITH JACK

I was saddened by my mother's death, but found the companionship and solace I needed in Jack. He was the perfect partner for older married life. He was adventurous and had a great sense of humor, but he also had a soft side to him which showed itself when he was listening to classical music or enjoying the natural world. We would pass many days drifting along on our pontoon boat. Although I didn't like to participate in the *actual* fishing, I was always happy to sit in the boat and busy myself with tatting, knitting, or reading while Jack waited for the fish to bite. The Springfield area has many lakes, and we didn't have to go far to be on the water.

Two of my favorite parks to visit were Bennett Springs State Park and Roaring River. In each place, we had access to a nice mix of trails, picnic tables, and lakes and rivers. It just goes to show that every part of the country has its treasures, if you just take the time to look. Roaring

River was the place the Norths had gone on family vacations for many years. Every July, we all met there to celebrate the birthdays of Jack and Becky. When it became too difficult for us to get there, the family would come to our house and we would go to a fancy restaurant instead for dinner.

Although it was hard for me to leave Champaign, I came to like Springfield, Missouri and began to think of it as home. Part of the settling-in process involved making new friends. I'll admit, it's not easy making friends later in life. As an adolescent, you can meet people at school; as a young adult you can meet other parents through your children. But how do you meet people when you're over sixty years old? Fortunately, a few elements came together that made things easier on me: Jack's old friends, the church, and a new bridge club.

Jack had grown up in the Springfield area and still had some friends from Springfield Central High School. One of his high school friends, Dick Stolp, was also a Methodist Minister who had served in Illinois. In fact, Jack had encouraged Dick to apply for a position in Illinois, since there were more vacancies there and more opportunities for growth.

Just like us, the time came for Dick and his wife, Sue, to retire and make a change. They had been considering moving to Florida, where their son had decided to move, but plans changed and the son ended up moving to North Carolina instead. Uncertain of what to do—and not convinced that they wanted to live in North Carolina—Dick called Jack, and they had a long talk about our decision to move to Springfield. By the end of the phone call, I think Dick was convinced to move back home! They moved to Springfield right after we did, and I was relieved to have a few friends in the area.

We saw the Stolps often, whether at church or through other events like dinner, dominoes, or Scrabble nights. They also convinced us to start volunteering at St. John's Hospital (later named Mercy Hospital). After twelve years of volunteering there, Jack and I eventually shifted over to Cox Hospital, which was closer to our home (and also attached to our clinic). Jack and I ended up volunteering for a total of twenty-two years. I worked the information desk, pushed wheelchairs, checked in patients, and did other odd jobs that were needed. Volunteering added another layer of activity to my life in Springfield, and I am grateful the Stolps encouraged us to sign up.

Despite the Stolp's friendship, it was still difficult to adjust to the newness of Springfield. I'm used to having a network of friends, not just a few. I'm a social person—I *need* companionship—and I don't say this to brag, but I've never had any trouble talking to people and making friends. Growing up, people were always in and out of our home, and that constant buzz continued during my time in Champaign. In Springfield, Missouri, I knew the neighbors on either side of us and across the street, but I didn't know the *neighborhood* like I had in my previous homes. Fortunately, we had the church…although it was difficult to select the right one.

At the time, there were fifteen Methodist churches in Springfield and we went to most of them, usually more than once. For a minister, it's hard to find another minister that you can tolerate listening to every Sunday! Jack was particular about who would meet his standards, but he eventually settled on Reverend Clayton Smith of Schweitzer United Methodist Church. When we walked in for the first time, it immediately felt like home. There was excellent music, friendly people, and outstanding ministers. This church would come to fill our lives with many happy memories and long-lasting friendships.

Jack and Clayton didn't agree on everything—Clayton was more conservative than Jack and that would come out occasionally during his sermons—but he and Jack became friends and would have long discussions together. Clayton's wife had also died, so Jack was able to provide a certain understanding that most other people did not have.

Once we had our church established, I breathed a sigh of relief. Finally, I had my church family again! I joined the United Methodist Women's group and began to feel like things were getting back to normal.

I did not, however, volunteer for any officer positions like I had in Champaign. After all those years of responsibility, I felt I had earned a break. I also did not become involved in a church choir until several years later, after Jack had died. I enjoyed sitting next to Jack during the service and didn't want to give that up.

The last piece of my social life was the bridge club. After having played bridge for several decades in Champaign, it seemed strange to not be a part of a bridge club in Springfield. We had been living in Missouri for nearly two years before I found a club (or really, before *it* found *me*) One day, while I was volunteering at St. John's hospital, one of the volunteers asked me if I played bridge. Their club was looking for a sub, and she wondered if I might fill in. I agreed and joined them at their next game. I can hold my own at a bridge table, and I proved I was worthy enough to be a part of the club. They invited me back and that was how I found a new bridge community, without even seeking it. Somehow, bridge has a way of sniffing me out!

Jack never was a big bridge player, but I didn't mind. We had a lot in common, but we were also just different enough to make life interesting. I had my collections of figurines and my handwork; Jack had his fishing and electronics. He was always playing with speakers, computers, and phones. He also had an extensive music collection and loved going out to see the Springfield Symphony, for which we had season tickets. When we weren't listening to live music, Jack was always playing something at home on his stereo, usually classical music by Mozart, Bach, or Vivaldi. He would upgrade his speaker system every year, if I let him! That's how much he loved all things audio.

I, on the other hand, couldn't be bothered with stereo systems or computers. I am not bad with technology (and managed to learn how to navigate a smart phone and an iPad at the age of ninety-four), but it's not a passion. Jack was always dabbling with the computer, trying different programs or learning how to navigate the internet, and I relied on him to do any computer-related tasks for me.

I also relied on Jack to deal with everything car-related. Me? I don't care much about buying new cars. I'll use the same car for years and years, until it wears out. Jack, however, was accustomed to getting a new leased car each year. Old habits are hard to break, and we had to go look at new cars every year in Springfield. I *hated* it. Eventually, I decided I would just stay home and trust him to pick out the car he wanted. It was a compromise that worked out well for both of us.

TRAVEL

One of the interests we continued to share was a love of travel. I get a thrill out of seeing new places, and every place I've traveled to has been interesting and exciting in its own way. Since we were both retired and all our kids had long since become adults, Jack and I did a lot of traveling. When we weren't traveling across the country to visit family members and old friends, we were taking off on church-sponsored trips to all corners of the world.

Every place I visited opened up my world just a little bit more and taught me things that I would have otherwise never learned. We traveled to Scandinavia, the Caribbean, Europe, Egypt, Israel, Argentina, Panama, Canada, and many more. In every country, I was always amazed by the generosity and kind-heartedness of people. We're not as different as we sometimes think we are. Most people on this earth simply want to live in peace, share meals with their family and friends, and enjoy themselves.

One of the most fascinating places we visited was Israel. Jack had made four or five trips there during his years as a pastor. Not only is it an important religious area, but Educational Opportunities had also built a college there. I only visited Israel once, but it made a lasting impact. It was amazing to see all the historical relics and Biblical sites like the Jordan River, Bethlehem, or the hill where Jesus had given his Sermon on the Mount. I spent my whole life reading about Israel in the Bible, so actually visiting it was like stepping foot into a fairytale. It seemed that everywhere we went had some kind of religious significance, from the Wailing Wall to Jericho. Unfortunately, since our last trip, tension has increased in Israel, and I don't think it's safe to travel there right now. We were lucky to visit when we did.

Luck is a good word for all our travels. Though we ran into a little bit of trouble here or there, most of the time we had no issues and were able to simply enjoy the adventure. There were, however, a few memorable incidences when things didn't go quite as smoothly as expected. While we were in Cairo, Egypt, I became so sick I couldn't go on one of the tours. I couldn't keep anything down and felt achy and weak. Though I hate to admit this, I'm pretty sure my sudden illness was caused by a raw turnip I had eaten at a restaurant.

I love raw vegetables and when I saw sliced turnips on a tray, I popped one in my mouth without thinking.

Jack saw me do it and said, "Did you just eat that?"

"Yes," I admitted.

"You shouldn't have eaten that. Who knows where those vegetables were washed."

Being as stubborn as I am, I waved him off and said, "It'll be fine."

It wasn't, of course, and the rest of our time in Egypt was pretty miserable for me. We made the best of it, though, and still had some interesting experiences there, including a wild ride with a cab driver who showed us around the city while the rest of the group was on a tour. Jack was charismatic and talkative; he could easily get just about anyone engaged in conversation, and this cab driver was no different. It wasn't long before the cabbie was telling us about how he had been a "guest" in prison for five months. This raised our eyebrows, but the man turned out to be very friendly, with a great sense of humor. He told us he "only" spoke five languages and had a sister who was a doctor. He then asked us about ourselves and wondered if we had any kids.

"Yes," Jack said. "We've been married a year, and we have six children."

The man dramatically flung his hands in the air (and off the steering wheel!) and exclaimed, "All at once?!"

And then there was the time in England when we were late getting back to the tour bus. Our friends, the Clinebells, were also on that tour, and Harriette and I got wrapped up in conversation and shopping. Jack urged us to make haste and get to the bus. "We're going to be late," he said. "This way."

"We can go this way," I insisted, gesturing down a narrow road. "It's a shortcut."

I'm not exactly known for my sense of direction, and Jack said, "I'll buy you two more Hummels for your collection if you're right and the bus is that way."

"Deal," I said.

We took the street I had pointed out and, lo and behold, the bus was waiting for us just a few blocks down. Jack shook his head, smiled, and said, "Well, I guess I owe you two more Hummels."

I smile every time I see those figurines. Each one is tied to a memory, and it's fun for me to recall their stories whenever I look at my collection.

Our trip to the U.K. was just one of many that we shared with Harriette and Paul Clinebell. They were our favorite traveling companions, and we went on many trips and excursions together. We went on a South American cruise together, journeyed up to Alaska twice, traveled to beautiful Costa Rica, and took one memorable trip across Canada by rail.

During our Canadian rail trip, we spent six days on a passenger train from Montreal to Vancouver. The four of us chatted, dined, played cards, and enjoyed the stunning scenery from our train car. I was amazed at the topography in Canada! The land would change from flat pine forests to steep mountains in the blink of an eye. It was all so rugged and beautiful. Along the way, we'd stop at different sites designated by the tour company—everything from a barbeque pit stop to the shores of Lake Geneva.

Every country we visited was a new adventure. Whether we were on an Education Opportunities trip, a cruise with the Clinebells, or simply traveling by ourselves, I always learned a lot about the people, food, and culture. We visited towering cathedrals in Germany, saw the majestic fjords in Scandinavia, watched belly dancing and ate purple Kalamata olives in Greece, and toured the elaborate system of locks and dams at the Panama Canal.

Closer to home, Jack and I once stayed overnight by the Grand Canyon on our way from Arizona to San Francisco. That night, we went out to eat at a restaurant and began to watch the 1989 World Series game on TV. Suddenly, the TV picture began to tip and whirl. A major earthquake was happening in San Francisco! I immediately called Ralph and Edith Baxter (Jake's brother and wife), who we had intended to visit in San Francisco, and they said, "Stay away!" So we improvised. Instead of risking San Francisco, we drove to Las Vegas and toured the Las Vegas strip, then traveled north and went fishing in Bozeman, Montana. Not such a bad trip, after all!

During our marriage, Jack and I visited many other North American destinations together. Retirement wasn't exactly a time of rest for us, but that's how we liked it. In many ways, my time with Jack was like a second life (or a third, if you count my widowhood). With Jake, I raised children and started my career; with Jack I traveled and enjoyed retirement.

ANOTHER LOSS

Though Jack and I had many nice, relaxing times together, life wasn't without its challenges. When you get married later in life, you have to expect to weather some health issues. Aside from our minor illnesses (my stomach troubles in Egypt or Jack getting sick in Nova Scotia from eating too many clams at the Harvard Senior Dinner!), we had to deal with a few serious scares, including Jack falling ill while we were visiting the Outer Banks of North Carolina. Without warning, his temperature rose, he couldn't keep anything down, and he became delirious with fever. I packed the R.V. and began driving toward home.

We hadn't made it far on our journey back to Missouri when we realized we had to stop. We pulled into the first hospital we could find in Ripley, West Virginia, and I brought Jack into the emergency room. They immediately hospitalized him and began treating his fever.

I stayed by his side most of the time, willing him to get better. The nurse and I bathed him all night with cold damp towels to bring his fever down. During this time, poor Jack wasn't all there. In his delirium, he would bring his hands to his chest and move his fingers together in delicate motions; we all decided he was tying lures for fly fishing in his sleep!

After two days, Jack's fever broke, and we all breathed a sigh of relief. Later, the doctor pulled me aside and confided, "When you brought him in here, I didn't think you'd be taking him home."

John and Kathy drove from Illinois to West Virginia to help, and I will always be grateful to them for coming. John returned to Illinois in Kathy's car, and Kathy and I drove the R.V. back to Illinois. After a couple of days there, I drove the R.V. and Jack back to Springfield. Jack never remembered any of this part of our trip!

Jack was tough and pulled out of his illness just fine. It wasn't long before he was back to doing all the things he liked to do—fishing, attending church, and listening to his beloved Mozart. Unfortunately, only a few years later he had to fight another battle—this one against kidney failure.

The two years that Jack was on dialysis were not easy. He was often tired and weak, but he kept in good spirits and insisted on carrying on with life as usual. After dialysis, he never wanted to go directly home, but instead chose to go out to eat—usually at one of his favorite restaurants called The Buzz.

I admire the way he persevered until the very end. When he was finally hospitalized and could no longer keep down food, the medical staff asked him whether or not he would like to use a feeding tube.

"No," Jack said, knowing full-well what that meant. Without receiving nourishment, the dialysis treatments would not be effective.

The physicians were wonderful and made Jack comfortable during those last few days. We all made peace with his decision and waited as patiently as we could by his side, trying to make his environment as soothing and relaxed as possible. We brought in a CD player so he could listen to Mozart, set up a few dimly lit lamps, and provided chairs for friends and relatives who visited. We quietly kept vigil at his bedside.

On January 20, 2010, with his four children at his side, Jack closed his eyes for the last time and left to meet the God he had served his entire life.

THE GARDENS

Life without Jack was strange. This time, I didn't have my daughters nearby or the comfort of my mother's presence. I had my church family, friends, and neighbors, but I still felt awfully alone living in that big house by myself. I had heard that it's best to not make any major changes during the first year after your spouse has died, so I decided to stay put and count the days until I could move out of that place and away from all the little reminders of Jack. His music collection, fishing poles, computer, stereo system—all of it could bring me to tears in an instant.

All six of our children made special trips to Springfield to help me with house repairs and yard work, even though it was a long trip for all of them. I had told my girls that when the time to move out of my house came, I hoped I would go gracefully (as opposed to kicking and screaming!). One day, Janie and Kathy told me they thought it was time for me to move, so together we began to look at independent living communities in the Springfield area.

I finally settled on The Gardens. It offered spacious rooms, beautiful grounds, exercise classes, a pool, and many other amenities that would be a welcome relief from running an entire house by myself. It wasn't that I minded moving, it was that the *thought* of moving was overwhelming. Janie and Kathy assured me that all I had to do was say I was ready, and they would take care of everything to get me moved.

True to their word, the six of our children worked together to sort, purge, donate, pack, and move my belongings to my new apartment at The Gardens. Becky, Mary, and Charlotte organized a garage sale, and Janie's friend, Phil, helped get the house ready to sell.

I was ready to give up homeownership and finally rest a little.

Rest, however, is relative. I've always been an active person, and at The Gardens, I went from being very active to slightly less active. I eventually played in not one, not two, but *three* bridge clubs. When I joined the first bridge group at The Gardens, it was like they were just *waiting* for their fourth player to arrive. After that, the word must have spread that I enjoyed bridge, because soon I was playing several times each week. I'll admit, after a while I was a little "bridged out."

The Gardens was a nice community, and I made several friends there and met many interesting people. One man in one of my bridge clubs had been a Prisoner of War during WWII, and it just so happened that another man at The Gardens was a former Army Colonel who had liberated the very camp in Poland where that POW had been imprisoned. This was just one of many incredible stories from the residents at The Gardens. I have learned that everyone has a story; you just have to let them tell it.

During this time, I continued to attend Schweitzer Church and became active with the Senior Saints, the church's choral group for senior citizens. There were about thirty of us, and we would sing at church once a month, or out in the community at nursing homes or assisted living facilities. All these activities were usually a welcomed distraction, but sometimes, I simply didn't feel like leaving my apartment. On those days, I would occasionally pull out Jack's sermons, read them, and sing hymns to myself. It was like having my own private service.

Sundays weren't the only times when I became keenly aware of Jack's absence. Whenever I had to turn to technology and try to figure it out on my own, I was reminded of him. I didn't think I'd ever need to learn how to use all that stuff, but I guess I was wrong. After Jack's death, I had to be brave enough to face my technology fears and learn how to operate a computer, a cell phone, and a Kindle. When I first started to learn how to operate a computer, I didn't even know how to turn it on! I like to say that I learned how to use it "by guess and by golly." Janie taught me a few things, and so did David, but a lot of what I've learned came by simply trying things. I recently learned how to use an iPhone and an iPad. It has been especially challenging to learn to use the touch screen; I use a stylus now, and I think I've gotten the hang of it. I can even use text messaging, play Words With Friends, and use FaceTime to chat with my children, grandchildren, or great-grandchildren.

I must get some of my adaptability from my mother. She was always trying new things, even into her eighties. Whether it was teaching herself how to use a typewriter, figuring out a new sewing technique, or helping me puzzle out a household repair, she was fearless when it came to trying something new.

TODAY

It's a good thing I have the "adaptable gene" because I've had to get used to a lot of changes in my life. I was only at The Gardens for six years when Janie and Kathy proposed another move. This time, Janie came armed with a spreadsheet of pros and cons for moving to

Minnesota. She was proposing that I get an apartment at Friendship Village in Bloomington, Minnesota in the same continuing care independent living community where she had been living for five months. The girls thought it would be nicer for me to live closer to family, and Janie thought I would do well there…in the bridge Mecca of Minnesota!

After much thought, prayer, and discussion, I agreed. Although I had friends in Springfield, I really didn't have any family there, and I missed being close to the girls. In Minnesota, I would be just a quick walk away from Janie and a short plane ride away from Kathy, who still lives in Illinois.

In June of 2017, Kathy, Linda, Mary, and Janie carefully packed my Hummels, my cup and saucer collection, my spoon collection, all the items I have tatted or knit over the years, my photographs, and my essentials. It's amazing to think that nearly ninety-five years of life could fit inside a single moving truck and my car. Once again, David, John, and Phil were at the ready for another move.

At Friendship Village, I had to adjust to a brand new life. I had Janie, but nothing else was familiar to me. I was starting over in a new city with new friends, a new church, a new doctor and dentist, a new phone number, and even a new bed! I had developed a routine at The Gardens, and now I had to carve out a new one.

It should come as no surprise that I quickly joined a couple of bridge clubs. Somehow, I have trouble saying no to bridge! I also joined a knitting group and have been working on a few projects, including tatting a decorative table cover to add to Janie's collection of items I have tatted for her.

This past October, I turned ninety-five. I was lucky to spend my birthday week with many family members and friends, from all over the country. My birthday week included lunch in Saint Paul with Janie, Kathy, and my niece, Leigh Ann Payne-Meili; lunch in Salt Lake City to visit Derek and his family and to see (for the first time) his new twin boys;

dinner in Bloomington with David, Linda, John, and Janie; lunch in Champaign with Harriette Clinebell, two of her children, Bob and Connie Atkins, John's wife, Mary, and Janie and Kathy. A grand birthday week, indeed.

My children and grandchildren seem to always go out of their way to shower me with kind gestures. For instance, my granddaughter, Samantha, gave me an exceptionally precious gift for my ninety-fifth birthday: the opportunity to work with a professional writer to record my memoir. And then there was the impromptu lunch trip to Salt Lake City…

Kathy and Janie told me the day before the trip that we would be going to Salt Lake City to visit my twin grandsons. They said I did not need to pack because it would be a quick trip, and we were going out and back the same day. What they did *not* tell me was that Kathy had chartered a private jet for the trip! Imagine my surprise and delight as we drove onto the tarmac, right to the nose of the plane, and walked on red carpet into the cabin. Kathy, her sister-in-law, Karen, Janie, and I spent a stress-free and fun plane ride to and from Salt Lake City! The only way to fly! Definitely one of the all-time highlights of my life.

Some people ask me what my secret is—how I've managed to stay relatively healthy and fit all the way to age ninety-five.

Well, I can't be certain, but it has to be a combination of things. Of course, genetics may play a part, but I also exercise regularly, eat well, never drink alcohol or coffee, get a weekly massage, and spend several hours each week in prayer and contemplation. It might also have something to do with my laid back attitude and my tendency to just go with the flow. Rather than resist, I let life take me where it wants me to go.

It was this kind of attitude that made me say "yes" to many different experiences that most people would never try. I waterskied up until the age of sixty-eight. I went up in a hot air balloon during grandson Derek's wedding celebrations when I was in my late eighties. I tried white water rafting for the first time before grandson Ben's wedding when I was ninety-one.

At the age of ninety-two, Ben called me on the phone and said, "How do you feel about sky diving?"

I hadn't thought much about it (besides thinking it was a lunatic thing to do!), but I said, "Well, I suppose if George Bush can do it as a senior citizen, I can too."

A friend of Ben's was going to take us, but that ended up falling through. We called several other sky diving companies, but no one was willing to take me. I was secretly a little relieved, although my thinking was: "Why not try sky diving? At my age, what do I have to lose?"

I have tried to approach life fearlessly. We're only given so much time on this earth, so why not make the most of it? Why not travel the world; experience new things; and devote yourself to friends, family, and God? Even though there were times in my life when I felt alone and afraid, I was always able to rise above those low points and step forward. Fearlessly, with God by my side.

Family Photos

My Grandparents

Sidney Morris Chapman and Sarah Jane Rea Chapman

James Dickason Dent, Sarah Elizabeth Parrack,
Willis David, Charles Hampton, Lillian Adrah

My Parents

Ella Irene Chapman Dent and Charles Hampton Dent

The Five Dent Children

Martha – Jane

Morris – Adrah – Charles Rea

Mother, Martha,
Jane, Charles Rea,
Adrah, Morris,
Daddy

Back: Jane , Mother,
Charles Rea, Daddy

Front: Adrah, Morris,
Martha

Our Montgomery Home

615 Fourth Avenue

Montgomery
Police Station

Daddy, Martha, & Jane

Jane & Martha in new
dresses made by Mother

Jane & Martha in our red wagon

Martha & Jane on the swing
in our front yard

Jane & Martha in
new coats and hats
made by Mother

< Charles Rea
in his Cub
Scout Uniform

Charles Rea in
typical knicker
fashion of the
day for boys >

Morris and Me beside Aunt Ruth's car

1940

In my high school band uniform with my new Silver King Clarinet (I planted the peach tree behind me from seed!)

Me, Cousin Esther, & Jane

Mr. McVey, the Jewel Tea Man, Me, & Esther

1940

My high school
graduation picture

Carl Hammond in front of his laundry truck

Carl and Me at Lover's Leap
at Hawk's Nest, West Virginia

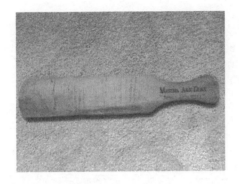

My Sigma Iota Chi Sorority Pledge Paddle

Dressed up to advertise the
Charlie Chaplin movie being
shown at the Avalon Theater

Jacob Robert Baxter
graduation from
college

Jake and Me in my front yard in Montgomery

Mr. & Mrs. Jacob R. Baxter
on our wedding day

1944 in New Haven Connecticut

Bike trip with New Haven friends

Jake at Savin Rock

Jake and Me, ready for a picnic
and swimming with friends

Jake at his work in New Haven

Jake and his friends

1943 – Me in Proctor, WV

1939 – Me by our house in
Montgomery in a blue corduroy
dress my mother made

Postcard from 1943 NYC Trip

Times Square, New York City.

Proctor, West Virginia

The Baxter
Home by
Proctor Creek

Jake's Parents:
Josephine and
Herman Baxter

Proctor Creek,
where Wilma took
the donkeys and
cows each day to
graze while she
walked up the hill
to teach school

The Baxter Family, 1955 – Back: Ralph, George,
Josephine, Jake, & Herman. Front: Wilma, & Faye

Left to Right:
Thelma Baxter,
Martha Baxter,
Faye Cook,
Betty Baxter

Champaign, Illinois

315 South Garfield Avenue

1945 – Janie and Me

1949 – Kathy and Me

1951 – Kathy & Janie in
dresses I made

1952 – Kathy & Janie

1954 – The Baxter Family, Easter Sunday

1950 – Me in a dress my
mother made for me

My bridge club in
Champaign that played
together for 40 years!

1942 bathing fashion! At a
Sigma Iota Chi Sorority
party at Beckwith, W.V.

1950 – Lake of the Woods
family picnic and swimming.
Steve Shoemaker and Me.
Janie and David Shoemaker
are in the background.

1959 – Jake
and Me in
Proctor, W.V.

1968 – Jake and Me on our way to dinner to
celebrate our twenty-fifth wedding anniversary

1976 – Kathy's wedding: Howard & Jane Meadows, my
Mother, Me, Kathy & Sam Anderson, Janie, Adrah & Don
Payne, Charles Rea, Aunt Lillian, Aunt Ruth

Springfield, Missouri

3934 Gatlin Court

Dr. & Mrs. Jack B. North
Our wedding day,
November 29, 1985

Our Wedding Party
Janie, David, Kathy,
Rev. Floyd Stradley,
Charlotte, Me,
Becky, Jack, & John

2015 – John & Mary, Becky, Charlotte, Me, Kathy, Janie, Linda & David

2009 – Jack & Me

2016 – Me in
my apartment
at The Gardens

Mother's first
wedding present
that I gave to
Derek & Stacy
for a wedding gift

The first cup in my
collection, which
has now been
divided between
Stacy and Samantha

2017 Bloomington, Minnesota

2017 – Kathy, Me, Janie

Kathy's family in Big Sky, M.T.
Eric, Alexandria, & Samantha Morales; Stacy, Samuel, Cora,
Derek, & Wesley Anderson; Freyja and Ben Anderson (right side)

85515598R00104

Made in the USA
Middletown, DE
24 August 2018